HAITI
in Pictures

VGS

Margaret J. Goldstein

Lerner Publications Company

Contents

Website address: www.lernerbooks.com

Lerner Publications Company
A division of Lerner Publishing Group
241 First Avenue North
Minneapolis, MN 55401 U.S.A.

Library of Congress Cataloging-Publication-Data

Goldstein, Margaret J.
    Haiti in pictures / by Margaret J. Goldstein.
      p. cm. — [Visual geography series]
    Includes bibliographical references and index.
    ISBN-13: 978-0-8225-2670-4 [lib. bdg. : alk. paper]
    ISBN-10: 0-8225-2670-0 [lib. bdg. : alk. paper]
    1. Haiti. 2. Haiti—Pictorial works. I. Title. II. Series: Visual geography series [Minneapolis, Minn.]
F1915.B44 2006
972.94—dc22   2004014794

Manufactured in the United States of America
1 2 3 4 5 6 – BP – 11 10 09 08 07 06

INTRODUCTION

Located on an island in the Caribbean Sea, Haiti is an intriguing yet deeply troubled country. In its two hundred years as an independent nation, it has been scarred by revolutions and natural disasters. Its government has rarely been stable, and its people have mostly been poor.

Culturally, however, Haiti is extremely rich. Most of its citizens are black—descendants of Africans shipped to the Caribbean to work as slave laborers in earlier centuries. At the same time, Haiti has a French heritage, because for many years France controlled the region that became modern-day Haiti. Haiti's main language, Creole, is a unique mixture of French, African, and other languages. Haiti's dominant religion, Vodou, is a faith with its roots in Africa. Although the Haitian people have struggled for centuries with poverty and civil strife, they have also made great achievements in literature and the arts. Haiti has produced many acclaimed painters, woodcarvers, and sculptors. Haitian music is famed worldwide.

Hispaniola (the island encompassing modern-day Haiti and the Dominican Republic) was originally home to Taíno Indians, Native Americans who made their living by fishing and farming. Christopher Columbus, the well-known Italian explorer, arrived in Hispaniola during his first voyage to the Western Hemisphere in 1492. Sponsored by the Spanish government, Columbus established a Spanish colony on Hispaniola. The colonists enslaved most of the Taíno Indians, who soon died of overwork, hunger, and disease.

Shortly afterward, France took control of the western half of Hispaniola. French colonists imported African slaves to work on their farms and build their cities. Led by François-Dominique Toussaint, the slaves rebelled against their French masters and established an independent nation, called Haiti, in 1804.

The following two hundred years were very difficult for Haiti. The nation could not establish a stable government, and its people grew desperately poor. Corrupt rulers looted its treasury and terrorized citizens.

CUBA

TORTUGA ISLAND

ATLANTIC OCEAN

Windward Passage

Port-de-Paix

NORD-OUEST

Les Trois River

Acule Bay

Cormien Beach

Cap-Haïtien

NORD

Sans Souci Palace

Citadelle Laferrière

The Citadel National Park

NORD-EST

Gonaïves

L'ARTIBONITE

Gulf of Gonâve

Artibonite River

Saint-Marc

CENTRE

Lake Péligre

GONÂVE ISLAND

Trou Caïman Lake

Lake Saumâtre

DOMINICAN REPUBLIC

Port-au-Prince Bay

OUEST

Jérémie

Macaya National Park

GRAND' ANSE

Miragoâne

Lake Miragoâne

Port-au-Prince ✪ Pétionville

La Visite National Park

Pine Forest National Park

SUD

Les Cayes

SUD-EST

Jacmel

CARIBBEAN SEA

Haiti

——— International border
– – – Department border
✪ Capital city
• City
■ Point of interest
∴ Archaeological ruin

0 ————— 40 Miles
0 ————— 40 KM

N

UNITED STATES

ATLANTIC OCEAN

FLORIDA

BAHAMAS

GREATER ANTILLES

DOMINICAN REPUBLIC

MEXICO

CUBA

JAMAICA

HAITI

PUERTO RICO

PACIFIC OCEAN

CARIBBEAN SEA

VENEZUELA

0 ————— 500 Miles
0 ————— 500 KM

Hurricane Jeanne caused severe flooding along Haiti's northern coast in 2004. The city of Gonaïves *(above)* was hardest hit. The destructive force of hurricanes and economic, political, and social turmoil have led many Haitians to flee their country for more than four decades.

Periodically, hurricanes struck Haiti, bringing death and destruction to an already troubled nation. Hungry for a better life, thousands of Haitians left their homeland, moving to other Caribbean nations as well as the United States.

In modern times, Haiti's future is uncertain. It remains the poorest nation in the Western Hemisphere. It lacks good health care, education, housing, and sanitation. Its economy is weak, and its government is chaotic. Yet what the Haitians lack in material wealth, they make up for in spirit and determination. All Haitians hope for a more prosperous future, and with international assistance and hard work, they might achieve their goals.

Visit www.vgsbooks.com for links to websites with additional information about Haitian refugees and U.S. policy toward them.

THE LAND

Haiti is a small nation in the West Indies, an island group in the Caribbean Sea (part of the Atlantic Ocean). Haiti occupies the western third of the island of Hispaniola, which it shares with the larger Dominican Republic to the east. With an area of 10,714 square miles (27,749 square kilometers), Haiti is only slightly larger than the U.S. state of Vermont.

When viewed from the air, Haiti resembles the mouth of a huge sea monster, with two large peninsulas jutting out to the west like jaws, enclosing the Gulf of Gonâve. Small Gonâve Island sits inside the gulf, looking something like the sea monster's tongue. An even smaller island, Tortuga, sits off Haiti's northern coast.

Haiti's jagged coastline measures 694 miles (1,117 km), with a border on the Atlantic Ocean in the north, the Caribbean Sea in the south, and the Gulf of Gonâve in between. The nation's boundary with the Dominican Republic on the east, running north-south, measures 223 miles (360 km).

The island nation of Cuba sits about 50 miles (80 km) northwest of Haiti. A channel called the Windward Passage runs between the two countries. Jamaica, another island nation, is located about 100 miles (161 km) to the southwest. Other nearby islands include the Bahamas, Puerto Rico, and the Virgin Islands. The U.S. city of Miami, Florida, is located some 700 miles (1,126 km) northwest of Haiti.

Geographic Regions

The Taíno Indians—Hispaniola's original inhabitants—called their land Haiti, or "land of mountains." The country lives up to its name. Three-quarters of Haiti is mountainous. The northernmost mountain region is the Massif du Nord (North Mountain Range), located on Haiti's northern peninsula. The Noires Mountains (Black Mountains) lie in the middle of the country. Along the southern peninsula stretch the Massif de la Hotte (Hood Mountain Range) and its eastern section, the Massif de la Selle (Saddle Mountain Range). Haiti's highest point is Mount la Selle (8,793 feet or 2,680 meters), located in the Massif de la Selle.

Between the mountain ranges lie several plains and valleys. The Artibonite River valley runs along the Artibonite River in central Haiti, while the Cul-de-Sac Plain is located north of the Massif de la Selle. The Central Plain sits northeast of the Noires Mountains, and the North Plain stretches along the upper coastline between the Massif du Nord and the Atlantic Ocean. About 70 percent of Haiti's people live on the nation's plains and valleys.

Rivers and Lakes

Rushing streams spring from Haiti's mountain slopes and form numerous rivers that cascade into the sea. The largest of these is the Artibonite River, which flows westward through the Artibonite River valley and empties into the Gulf of Gonâve. On the river's eastern end, engineers have built a dam, creating artificial Lake Péligre. Water stored in the lake is used for irrigating (watering) crops, and water rushing over the dam creates hydroelectric power for Haiti's cities. The Les Trois River, which runs north to the Atlantic Ocean, is another large river in Haiti.

Haiti has several natural lakes. The largest is Lake Saumâtre, covering about 70 square miles (181 sq. km) and situated on the Dominican

A Haitian villager walks with his pack animal near **Lake Saumâtre.**

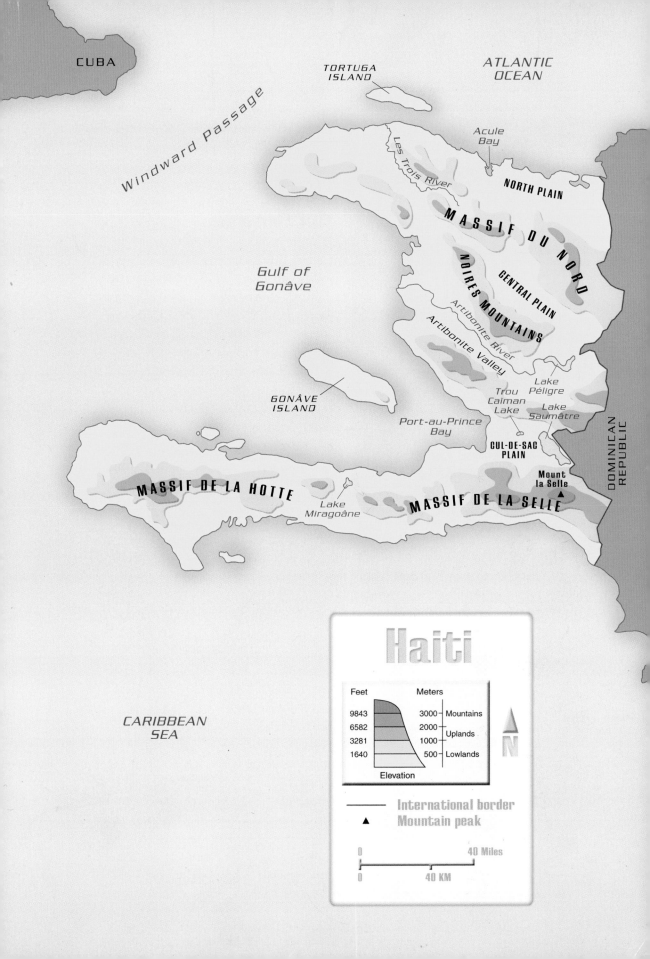

CUBA

ATLANTIC
OCEAN

TORTUGA
ISLAND

Windward Passage

Acule
Bay

Les Trois River

NORTH PLAIN

M A S S I F   D U   N O R D

*Gulf of
Gonâve*

CENTRAL PLAIN

NOIRES MOUNTAINS

Artibonite River

Artibonite Valley

Lake
Péligre

Trou
Caiman
Lake

Lake
Saumâtre

GONÂVE
ISLAND

Port-au-Prince
Bay

CUL-DE-SAC
PLAIN

DOMINICAN
REPUBLIC

Mount
la Selle

MASSIF DE LA HOTTE

Lake
Miragoâne

MASSIF DE LA SELLE

CARIBBEAN
SEA

Haiti

Feet	Meters	
9843	3000	Mountains
6582	2000	Uplands
3281	1000	
1640	500	Lowlands

Elevation

N

—— International border
▲ Mountain peak

0   40 Miles

0   40 KM

PROBLEMS UPON PROBLEMS

Hurricane Jeanne, which hit Haiti, in September 2004, was made worse by Haiti's extensive deforestation. Tree trunks, branches, and roots normally help absorb the blow of heavy hurricane rains. The water then slowly filters into the soil below. But because Haiti has been stripped of most of its forests, hurricane rains pound directly into the earth, washing away soil and causing floods and mudslides. Thousands of Haitian people died or were left homeless by flooding from Hurricane Jeanne.

border east of the capital city of Port-au-Prince. Near the middle of the southern peninsula is Lake Mira-goâne, covering about 10 square miles (26 sq. km). Other, smaller lakes are scattered throughout the nation.

◉ Climate

Haiti's climate is tropical, which means it features high temperatures and year-round rainfall. Along the coasts, temperatures range from lows around 68°F (20°C) to highs around 95°F (35°C), with less than 10 degrees variation between summer and winter. The capital city of Port-au-Prince, which sits just 120 feet (37 m) above sea level, has a yearly average temperature of 79°F (26°C). The air is cooler in the mountains, however, ranging from lows around 50°F (10°C) to highs around 75°F (24°C). In winter, frosts can occur high in the mountains.

Haitians divide their year into dry and rainy periods. Rainy seasons occur from April to June and from August to October. During these seasons, rain falls almost every day. May is one of the rainiest months in Haiti, with an average rainfall of nearly 10 inches (25 centimeters) in Port-au-Prince. Dry seasons occur in between rainy seasons. Depending on the location, Haiti can receive between 20 to 100 inches (50 to 254 cm) of rain each year.

Because of its location in the Caribbean Sea, Haiti is prone to hurricanes, giant swirling storms that form in the Atlantic Ocean. The hurricane season lasts from June through October, with July, August, and September being the most likely months for hurricanes. On September 17 and 18, 2004, Hurricane Jeanne slammed into Hispaniola, with winds clocked at 100 miles (161 km) per hour. Haiti was hit hard, especially the northwestern region around the city of Gonaïves. Almost 3,000 people lost their lives in the storm, which caused severe flooding and

Haiti is prone to be hit by earthquakes as well as hurricanes. In 1842 a large quake nearly destroyed Cap Haïtien.

Among Haiti's variety of plant life is **the date palm** (center).

mudslides. The storm left thousands more injured and hundreds of thousands homeless.

Flora and Fauna

Haiti boasts a wide variety of trees and flowers. Stately royal palm trees, which can reach heights up to 60 feet (18 m), lend an elegant air to many of the wide avenues of Port-au-Prince. Graceful coconut palms line many of the island's long waterfronts. High in the mountains, forests contain pine, mahogany, cedar, and rosewood trees, although vast areas of forest have been cut down in recent years. Some island trees yield edible fruits, such as avocados, mangoes, oranges, papayas, bananas, and coconuts. In some areas, beautiful orchids tumble from the trees in great scented clusters. Huge orange and red royal poincianas grow in great abundance, as do jasmine-scented frangipani, with their soft, velvety blossoms shaped like stars.

Haiti is home to scorpions, spiders, centipedes, and insects. Crocodiles and alligators live in lakes and in the shallow waters along

Haiti's **rhino-horned iguana.** The future of this reptile is uncertain because its habitat is rapidly vanishing in Haiti.

the Haitian coast. Rhino-horned iguanas, lizards, and snakes (none of them poisonous) live in Haiti too. Except for small rodents, few mammals are native to—or found originally in—Haiti. The nation does have a great many birds, including parrots and guinea hens. Inland lakes provide a haven for egrets, flamingos, migrating ducks, and other birds. Sea turtles, tuna fish, sardines, marlins, barracudas, tarpons, bass, and rock lobsters swim in the ocean waters.

Natural Resources

Haiti has a variety of mineral resources. Copper, manganese, gold, and silver come from the Massif du Nord. The Central Plain has deposits of lignite, a kind of coal. Other minerals found in Haiti include iron, lead, zinc, nickel, sulfur, marble, and gypsum. Haiti once had large deposits of bauxite (used to make aluminum), but its bauxite mines had been emptied by the late 1900s.

Haiti's trees are another valuable resource. Loggers cut down pine, mahogany, cedar, and other trees from Haiti's forests. The timber is used to make furniture, houses, and other products. Many Haitians cut down trees for firewood. Haiti's rushing rivers are also a natural resource. By damming the rivers that run through the mountains, Haitians can produce valuable electricity.

About 28 percent of Haiti's land is arable, or suitable for farming. Farmers grow sugarcane, cotton, rice, fruits, nuts, coffee, and other crops. Many farmers grow cacao beans, which are made into chocolate. Others raise livestock, such as cattle, goats, and pigs. The fish that swim in the waters around Haiti are another natural resource. Commercial fishers haul in millions of pounds of sea creatures each year. The catch is then processed and sold as food.

Environmental Issues

When it comes to environmental protection, Haiti has a poor track record. Because Haiti's government has been weakened by political turmoil, the nation has not passed strong environmental laws. What's more, it is a very poor country, without up-to-date or widespread sanitation systems. In many poor communities, people use rivers as sewers, polluting them with human and household waste. People have also polluted the ocean by dumping trash along the coast. All this pollution hurts and often kills the plants and animals that make their homes in and near the water.

Haiti once had a very lush landscape. But over the decades, Haitians have cut down most of the nation's forests for timber or to clear land for farms and houses. People have also cut down trees to use as firewood and charcoal (fuel made from charred wood), because many Haitians, especially the poorest citizens, have no other fuel available for cooking and heating. Haitians have planted few trees to replace those that have been cut down. As a result, many hillsides in Haiti are bare and lifeless. Without tree roots to hold the soil in place, soil washes away in the rain (a process known as erosion), clogging up rivers with mud. What's more, as people cut down Haiti's forests, the birds and other animals that make their homes there have fewer places to live.

Finally, people in Haiti have hurt animals by illegal hunting or too much fishing. When pollution and loss of habitat (natural homes) are added into the equation, many animals in Haiti have become endangered, or likely to die out altogether. At-risk animals include whales, seals, dolphins, manatees, crocodiles, iguanas, sea turtles, and many kinds of birds.

To protect its remaining wild lands and animals, Haiti has established four national parks: La Visite National Park, south of Port-au-Prince; Macaya National Park on the southern peninsula; Pine Forest National Park in the eastern Massif de la Selle; and Historic Citadel National Park in the Massif du Nord. These parks are off-limits to hunters, loggers, and land developers. But because of poor funding, park staff can't always enforce the rules. Still, visitors to the parks can enjoy areas of unspoiled rain forests, waterfalls, and meadows filled with wild plants and animals.

Cities

Haiti's coastline is punctuated by broad, deep bays, which have long served as seaports. Most of Haiti's major cities are located on these bays. Roughly 21 percent of Haiti's people live in urban areas. The biggest cities are Port-au-Prince (the capital) and Cap Haïtien. Smaller cities include Jacmel, Gonaïves, Jérémie, Les Cayes, Miragoâne, Port-de-Paix, and Saint-Marc.

Haiti's capital, **Port-au-Prince.** This aerial photograph offers a view of the city from Port-au-Prince Bay, looking south. The Massif de la Selle is in the background.

PORT-AU-PRINCE Located at Port-au-Prince Bay, at the easternmost edge of the Gulf of Gonâve, Port-au-Prince is Haiti's capital and largest city. It has an estimated population of 2 million. The city was founded in 1749 and was named for the *Prince,* a French ship anchored in the bay. It served as the capital of Saint Domingue, the original French colony on Hispaniola, and remained the Haitian capital after independence.

Modern Port-au-Prince mixes old and new, rich and poor. Dazzling white government offices share the streets with makeshift homes made of metal, brick, cardboard, and mud. Many roads are unpaved and strewn with garbage. Others are wide, paved avenues. The suburb of Pétionville is home to the city's wealthiest residents, while the poorest citizens make their homes in the shantytowns of Cité Soleil and Bel Air. Beggars are a common sight on city streets.

The heart of town is the Champs de Mars, a large park built in 1953. The park contains museums, monuments, and the National Palace, which serves as government headquarters. The city also bustles with open-air food markets, nightclubs, street festivals, and colorful murals.

CAP HAÏTIEN, a seaport on the northern coast, is Haiti's second largest city, with roughly 100,000 inhabitants. Located at the foot of the Massif du Nord, the city was founded by French settlers in 1670. Its original name was Cap-François.

During the French colonial years, wealthy French planters made their homes in the city. The surrounding countryside housed thriving sugar and coffee plantations—large farms worked by slave labor.

Cap-François was also the center of the slave uprising that brought slaves their freedom in the early nineteenth century. Jean-Jaques Dessalines defeated the French at Vertières, just south of the city, in the final battle for independence. Afterward, Dessalines changed the city's name to Cap Haïtien.

Modern Cap Haïtien has a number of impressive sites, specifically the Citadel, a giant fortress, and Sans Souci, a palace, both built by Henri Christophe, who ruled the northern part of Haiti in the early 1800s. Some beautiful beaches are located near the city. Offshore, divers can explore French, Dutch, and Spanish shipwrecks from the days of European colonization. Like Port-au-Prince, Cap Haïtien is also home to many slum neighborhoods.

JACMEL, although not one of the largest cities in Haiti, is certainly one of the most inviting. With a population of 15,000, it is a sleepy seaport town graced by nearby Caribbean beaches.

The city was originally a Taíno Indian settlement, then a French colonial town. It was also an important battleground during the fight for Haitian independence. After a fire destroyed the city center in 1896, the city was rebuilt with distinctive architecture, featuring wrought-iron balconies and graceful Victorian facades—similar to buildings seen in New Orleans, Louisiana, and other cities with a French heritage.

In modern times, Jacmel has become something of an artists' community, home to many painters and craftspeople. Jacmel's Carnival, or Mardi Gras celebration, is one of the most splendid in all of Haiti.

Visit www.vgsbooks.com, where you'll find links to photographs and information on current weather conditions, the most up-to-date population figures and other statistics, places to explore, and other items of interest.

HISTORY AND GOVERNMENT

Haiti's first inhabitants were Native Americans—people whose ancestors had lived in the Americas for thousands of years. Around 2600
B.C., people living in modern-day Venezuela in South America left
their homes, traveling northward in canoes to Hispaniola and other
Caribbean islands. The early settlers on Hispaniola made their homes
in caves and along riverbanks. They got their food by fishing in the
island's rivers and gathering wild plants.

About two thousand years later, another group of Native
Americans, also from Venezuela, arrived in the West Indies. Historians
call this group the Saladoids, because they probably came from
Saladero, Venezuela. Known as excellent potters, the Saladoids settled
on Hispaniola and other islands in the West Indies.

A third group of travelers came to Hispaniola and other Caribbean
islands during the first century B.C. Some historians think these travelers came from the South American nation of Peru, while others
think they, too, came from Venezuela. Calling themselves Taínos, or

"friendly people," these settlers gradually became the dominant group in the West Indies.

▶ Island Life

The Taínos on Hispaniola developed a rich culture, with complex systems of farming, government, and religion. They lived in permanent villages, with up to two thousand residents each. People built houses out of wooden poles and roofs made of thatch (grasses and other plant material). Groups of houses circled a village plaza. Groups of villages allied themselves with one another to create districts. Districts in turn joined together to form regions. Chiefs—whose power was inherited (passed down from one generation to the next)—ruled the villages, districts, and regions.

The Taínos were skilled farmers, growing cassava (an edible root), corn, sweet potatoes, yams, peppers, beans, squash, peanuts, and fruits such as guava and pineapple. They also grew tobacco, which they smoked by rolling up tobacco leaves to form a kind of cigar. The Taínos fished in rivers and the ocean using nets, spears, traps, and hooks. They made baskets, clay pottery, and gold jewelry. They used a plant fiber called sisal to make strong hammocks, which served as their beds. Because of the hot tropical climate, Taíno men wore only loincloths (aprons around the waist), and women wore only short skirts. The Taínos made their clothing out of cotton and palm fibers.

The Taínos worshipped many gods and spirits. People believed these spirits lived in trees, mountains, rivers, and other natural elements on which people depended for survival. The most important Taíno gods were Yúcahu, the god of cassava and the sea, and Atabey, goddess of freshwater and fertility.

Outsiders in the West Indies

By the late 1400s, approximately 400,000 Taínos were living on Hispaniola. At least 1 million more lived on neighboring islands in the Caribbean. For the most part, the Taínos' lives were peaceful. Occasionally, however, warlike people called the Caribs, based on islands to the east, attacked Taíno settlements. The Carib raiders killed Taíno men and captured Taíno women as slaves.

Then, in 1492, the Taíno on Hispaniola and other Caribbean islands encountered a different group of outsiders. In August of that year, Christopher Columbus, an Italian explorer, had set out from Spain to seek a western ocean passage to Asia, called the Indies at the time. His expedition included three ships: the *Pinta, Niña,* and *Santa María.*

This image shows the arrival of **Christopher Columbus** *(left, center)* at Hispaniola in 1492. Taíno people greet Columbus with offerings of food, unaware that he was claiming their lands for Spain.

On October 12, Columbus's crew spotted land. They had arrived at the Caribbean island of Guanahani (modern-day San Salvador, one of the islands of the Bahamas). The local Taíno people paddled out in boats to meet Columbus's ships. Columbus wasn't sure where he was. At the time, no Europeans knew that the Americas even existed. Thinking he had reached the Indies (Asia), Columbus called the islanders *indios*—or Indians. Europeans soon began using this name to refer to all native people in the Americas.

Columbus sailed on, exploring the northern coast of modern-day Cuba. In early December, the expedition reached another large island. Columbus called it La Isla Española (the Spanish Isle), a name that later became Hispaniola. Columbus was excited about the islands he had encountered, especially because some of the native people there wore gold jewelry. Columbus was hopeful that the islands would yield vast deposits of gold.

Spanish Settlements

On the night of December 24, 1492, Christmas Eve, the *Santa María* was wrecked on coral reefs off modern-day Cap Haïtien. The local Taíno people paddled out to help the struggling sailors and to collect the ship's wreckage, carrying the heavy timbers ashore. From these

timbers, Columbus built a wooden fort. He then sailed on, leaving thirty-nine men at the fort and ordering them to look for gold nearby.

Columbus returned to Spain, where he organized a second, larger expedition to the Americas. In September 1493, he left Cadiz, Spain, with a fleet of seventeen ships and 1,200 men. Returning to the fort on Hispaniola, Columbus found that Taínos had killed all thirty-nine of the Spanish settlers there. The Taínos had acted out of vengeance, because the Europeans had been kidnapping and raping Taíno women.

Columbus sailed his fleet farther east along Hispaniola's north coast and established a new settlement, called La Isabela—named after Queen Isabella of Spain. Leaving a group of colonists there, Columbus continued on to explore the southern coast of Cuba.

Within a year and a half, epidemics of disease swept through La Isabela, a fire destroyed most of its buildings, and a hurricane hit, doing more damage. So Columbus had another settlement built, this time on the island's southern coast. Led by Columbus's brother Bartolomé, the settlement survived. Originally called Nueva Isabela (New Isabella), it was later named Santo Domingo (and became the capital of the modern-day Dominican Republic). Columbus, meanwhile, continued to explore the Americas. On a third voyage, in 1498, he reached the northern coast of South America. On a fourth and final voyage, he explored the Central American coast.

The Spanish indeed found deposits of gold on Hispaniola. To extract the valuable mineral, they enslaved the native Taínos, forcing them to mine the gold under the most brutal conditions. All Taíno males over the age of fourteen had to work as miners. If they didn't extract enough gold, the Spaniards sometimes cut their hands off. Overworked, poorly fed, and brutalized, many Taínos died of starvation and exhaustion. Others died of diseases brought to the island by Europeans. By 1508 the island's Taíno population had fallen from about 400,000 to just 60,000. Ten years later, less than 3,000 Taínos remained alive on Hispaniola. Those who could escape—about 500 Taínos—fled to the mountains.

By the 1520s, Europeans realized that Columbus had not reached Asia on his voyages but instead had come upon the Western Hemisphere—called the New World—an area that had been entirely unknown to Europeans. European explorers, merchants, and settlers ventured to North, South, and Central America, seeking riches such as gold and silver, farmland, and other natural resources. They were eager to build settlements in the New World, establish ports and shipping routes, and map the unknown wilderness.

The Spanish used Hispaniola as a base of operations for further explorations in the Americas. By then the island's gold supplies had all been depleted, and Spanish colonists began to raise cattle and sugarcane on the island. With the Taínos almost entirely wiped out, the Spanish were desperate for more laborers. They began to import African slaves to Hispaniola.

France Arrives—and Stays

Pirates also operated in the New World. Pirates were outlaw sailors who raided merchant ships headed back to Europe with gold, silver, and other treasures from the New World. Some pirates, called privateers, operated with the backing of their governments in Europe—a tactic that allowed nations to damage their enemies' business ventures.

By 1630 French and British privateers had taken control of Tortuga Island, off the northern coast of Haiti. Using Tortuga as a base, the privateers raided Spanish merchant fleets filled with riches from Central and South America. These raids weakened Spanish control in

Hispaniola. In 1641 English and French privateers founded a settlement on the western end of Hispaniola. French colonists arrived to farm the surrounding land and soon became the dominant force in the region.

In 1655 England tried to take over all of Hispaniola, but Spanish defenders repelled the English attack. The French had more luck, at least in western Hispaniola. In 1664 France's King Louis XIV placed the western part of the island under control of the French West India Company, a private business. Bertrand d'Ogeron, a former pirate, was made governor of the territory.

In 1697, as part of an agreement called the Treaty of Ryswick, Spain gave the western third of Hispaniola to France. This deal left the eastern two-thirds of the island, known then as Santo Domingo (the modern-day Dominican Republic), under Spanish control. France called its new colony Saint Domingue (known in modern times as Haiti).

Under French rule, Saint Domingue quickly prospered. Using the labor of black slaves shipped from Africa, French settlers cut timber from Saint Domingue's forests. They created huge plantations for growing sugarcane, coffee, cacao, and cotton. Settlers also built roads, fine houses, and irrigation systems—networks of ditches and pumps that carry water to crops.

Tortuga means "Turtle" in Spanish. Tortuga Island got its name because its rounded shape resembles a turtle shell.

This folk art painting shows enslaved African people aboard **a slave ship.** The French and Spanish brought African slaves to Hispaniola to work on plantations there, starting in the 1500s. Most of Haiti's population is descended from Africans.

This illustration shows **a mulatto woman *(center)* and two slaves** in French colonial Hispaniola. Mulattoes—people of mixed European and African descent—were free persons, holding a greater status than slaves.

The French established towns such as Cap-François and Port-au-Prince. They also brought their major religion, Roman Catholicism, to Haiti. They built grand churches and taught Catholic practices to their slaves.

Racial Divides

Soon Saint Domingue was France's richest colony. More settlers arrived in the colony. Plantation owners imported more and more African slaves to work their lands. By the late eighteenth century, Saint Domingue had a population of about 500,000 black slaves, 30,000 whites, and 27,000 mulattoes—or people of mixed race.

White people (mostly French plantation owners and businesspeople) had almost all the power in the colony. They held high government positions, owned large estates, and ran businesses. They had the same rights and freedoms as French citizens living in France.

Black people, who made up the vast majority of the colony's residents, were enslaved—they had no rights or freedoms. Most slaves worked on large plantations, where they often endured brutal treatment at the hands of their masters. Although taught the Catholic beliefs of their French masters, Haitian slaves maintained a distinctive culture. They had brought their their own languages and traditions with them from Africa. Many practiced Vodou, a religion with its roots in western Africa.

Mulattoes occupied a middle ground. Officially, the French government considered them free people and French citizens. Many owned plantations and slaves. Some sent their children to school in France. However, Saint Domingue's French white elite tried to limit the rights and status of mulattoes. White authorities passed laws barring mulattoes from carrying guns, holding political office, and holding jobs as priests, lawyers, doctors, and teachers. Mulattoes had to attend separate churches and theaters from whites, and even had to wear a different style of clothing.

The mulattoes grew angry. In 1789 they heard about the French Revolution, during which French citizens rose up against their king and demanded more rights from their government. Inspired by this event, the mulattoes also demanded equal rights as French citizens. In early 1791, a young mulatto named Vincent Ogé led a protest against the government. He was arrested and put to death.

But the hostilities continued to simmer. Not just the mulattoes but also the slaves wanted equality. In August 1791, Saint Domingue's slaves joined the mulatto revolt, demanding freedom from their masters. In a violent uprising, slaves lashed out at their masters, burning plantations and killing both whites and mulattoes. Fearing for their lives, many whites and mulattoes fled Saint Domingue. François-Dominique Toussaint, a self-educated former slave, became a leader in the slave revolt, leading an army of black forces against the French.

In this illustration, slaves and mulattoes rebel against the French at Saint Domingue in 1791. That year, the two groups joined forces to fight for liberty and equality.

NAME CHANGE

As a soldier, François-Dominique Toussaint earned the nickname Toussaint-Louverture (the opening), a name that referred to his ability to find an opening in the enemy lines, as well as his opening the way for Haitian independence.

○ Toussaint Takes Charge

On the eastern portion of Hispaniola —still controlled by Spain—Spanish colonists supported the slave and mulatto revolt. They hoped the revolt would undermine French control and give Spain a chance to retake all of Hispaniola. Great Britain, too, saw an opportunity to regain a foothold in Saint Domingue. Both Spain and Britain sent in armies to claim the colony's burned-out plantations.

France's government, already weakened by the revolution at home, was unable to send enough soldiers to put down the slave rebellion or defeat the foreign invaders. So the French government decided to appease—make peace with—the black rebels. It granted the slaves of Saint Domingue their freedom in 1793. Then it enlisted the former slaves to help fend off the Spanish and British invasion.

So Toussaint and his men switched sides. Fighting suddenly under the French flag, they successfully pushed back the Spanish and British invaders. In October 1795, Spain admitted defeat. It signed a treaty granting all of Hispaniola to France, although many Spaniards remained living on the eastern part of the island.

François-Dominique Toussaint lies dying in a French prison in this image from the early 1800s. Threatened by Toussaint's rise to power and his support for Haitian independence, the French imprisoned Toussaint in 1802.

With French approval, Toussaint became the new ruler of Saint Domingue. He first drafted a constitution that banned slavery in the colony. He then invaded the Spanish portion of Hispaniola, declared all of Hispaniola to be an independent nation, and named himself president for life.

Once supportive of Toussaint, the French government grew angry with the brash new leader. Napoleon Bonaparte, who had seized power in France, sent a huge army under the command of his brother-in-law, General Charles Leclerc, to subdue Toussaint and restore slavery on Hispaniola. Against the powerful Leclerc, Toussaint's resistance was short-lived. He tried to negotiate a peace treaty, but instead of negotiating, Leclerc took him captive and sent him to prison in France in 1802. He died there a year later.

Independence

Enraged over the betrayal that had placed Toussaint in chains and fearful of the restoration of slavery, three of Toussaint's generals—Henri Christophe, Jean-Jacques Dessalines, and Alexandre Pétion—regrouped their followers. They were determined to abolish slavery forever and to declare Saint Domingue's independence from France. Fighting continued.

Henri Christophe

Initially, the French forces had great success. They captured Port-au-Prince and the southern provinces. Christophe's forces burned Cap Haïtien —to prevent it from falling to Leclerc's troops— and then fled. Of the three generals, only Dessalines, based in the northwest, was able to hold off the French. In late 1802, however, Leclerc and many of his troops died of a disease called yellow fever. The new French general was Donatien Rochambeau, who had been Leclerc's second in command. Greatly weakened by yellow fever and short on troops, the French forces no longer fought ably. On November 18, 1803, Dessalines defeated Rochambeau at the Battle of Vertières, and the French surrendered.

On January 1, 1804, Dessalines again proclaimed independence for Hispaniola, declaring the birth of a new nation called Haiti, the original Taíno name for the island. Dessalines, a former slave born in western Africa, gave himself the title Emperor Jacques I.

A Divided Nation

Although initially a hero to his people, Dessalines ruled cruelly. He ordered his soldiers to kill most of the white French people who remained in the country, and he forced most of the blacks to work on plantations—much as they had when they were slaves. The nation's mulattoes, a minority of the population but the educated and governing classes, were alarmed. During a mulatto uprising in October 1806, troops loyal to mulatto general Alexandre Pétion killed Dessalines.

Following the killing, Henri Christophe and Alexandre Pétion struggled for power. Christophe, who like Dessalines was a former slave, took control of the northern part of the country. He established a capital at Cap Haïtien, where he proclaimed himself king of Haiti in 1807. Christophe ruled with an iron fist, limiting people's freedoms, yet he also made some improvements in Haitian society. He established the nation's currency (money) system, built up the navy, opened schools, constructed several palaces, and built the magnificent fortress, Citadelle Laferriére (the Citadel).

Alexandre Pétion

In the south, mulatto leaders elected Alexandre Pétion to succeed Dessalines. Based in Port-au-Prince, Pétion called himself a president, not a king. He tried to run his portion of the nation democratically, with freedom for all citizens. He was a popular leader who distributed land to former slaves, but his section of Haiti did not prosper during his rule.

Neither leader controlled the eastern portion of Hispaniola. That area remained home to many Spaniards, who wanted their region to rejoin Spain as a colony. Having been defeated in the west, France made a slight effort to hang onto this part of Hispaniola, but with no success. The eastern part of the island returned to Spanish control in 1808.

Haiti Falls into Chaos

Pétion died in 1818. Jean-Pierre Boyer, a wealthy mulatto, was elected president to succeed Pétion in the south. In the meantime, Christophe had grown distraught over a rebel uprising in his territory, and he took his own life in 1820. Boyer assumed control of northern Haiti upon Christophe's death, thus unifying the nation.

In eastern Hispaniola, colonists revolted against Spain in 1821. Boyer took advantage of the turmoil there to conquer that part of the island. With the help of a strong army, Haiti ruled over all of Hispaniola for twenty-two years. Tensions grew between the mostly black Haitians in the west and the Spanish-descended Dominicans, as they were called, in the east.

By 1843 the Haitian people were unhappy with Boyer's government, which they accused of corruption and mishandling the nation's economy. Facing a rebellion, Boyer fled to Jamaica and then Paris. With the Haitian government in turmoil and unable to control the whole island, the neighboring Dominicans declared their independence from Haiti a year later, establishing the Dominican Republic.

The turmoil continued in Haiti—with ongoing conflict between the nation's majority blacks and minority mulattoes. Neither group wanted to let the other gain power. The country was rocked by rebellions, revolutions, and civil wars. Time after time, opposition groups toppled governments, assassinating some presidents and forcing others into exile (out of the country). Although the nation had written rules for elections and lawmaking, the various political factions ignored the rules, instead using violence to seize and enforce power.

Between 1843 and 1915, Haiti had twenty-two heads of state. Although a few leaders made small improvements to the nation's farms and roads during this era, none was able to bring stability to the country or heal the deep divisions between racial groups. At the same time, foreign businesses, especially U.S. businesses but also some British, German, and French companies, began to invest in Haitian plantations, banks, and railroads. Immigrants from the Middle Eastern nations of Syria and Lebanon also came to Haiti to set up businesses.

U.S. Intervention

By 1915 Haiti's economy was in ruins. Most of its people were uneducated and desperately poor. Peasant farmers raised just enough food for their own family use, but with none left over to sell. Clothing, housing, and health care were all substandard. The Haitian government also owed vast amounts of money to foreign countries.

The United States, the largest powerful country near Haiti, was concerned about the political and economic upheaval there. The nation held a strategic position on the Windward Passage, an important shipping lane. It was also near the newly opened Panama Canal, a shipping channel through Central America that linked the Atlantic and Pacific oceans. The United States wanted to make sure that the violence in Haiti didn't disrupt U.S. trade, specifically businesses and merchant shipping there.

In 1915, during yet another violent political upheaval, the United States sent a force of marines to occupy Haiti and protect U.S. business interests. The marines also came to make sure that Germany, a U.S. enemy in World War I (1914–1918), didn't establish a naval base in Haiti.

Signing a treaty with Haiti, the United States took complete control of Haiti's government and economy. It appointed government officials, wrote a new constitution; built schools, roads, sewers, telephone systems, and health clinics; and boosted the sagging economy with loans. It also allowed U.S. companies to buy vast amounts of land in Haiti.

Many Haitians resented U.S. control of their nation. Haitian blacks were particularly angry that the United States dealt almost entirely with mulattoes in its governing of the country, ignoring the black majority. Haitians staged a series of rebellions against U.S. rule from 1918 to 1920, but U.S. troops brutally suppressed the rebels, killing several thousand of them.

Soon after, educated black Haitians spearheaded a movement for black pride. Called Négritude (meaning "Africanness"), the movement encouraged Haitians to reject French culture and to embrace their African heritage and black identities. The Négritude movement was coupled with the Noirisme (blackness) movement, which called for taking power from the mulatto minority and transferring it to the black majority.

Self-Rule Restored

By 1930 the United States was ready to return self-government to Haiti. Haiti was no longer of much strategic importance to the United States, and U.S. control had been costly. With the help of the United States, in 1930 Haitians elected a national assembly (congress), which chose Sténio Vincent, a mulatto, as president. In 1934 the United States pulled the marines out of Haiti, but the U.S. government kept direct control of Haiti's finances until 1941.

Vincent's term ended in 1941, and Elie Lescot, another mulatto, succeeded him as president, again chosen by the national assembly. Lescot's term ended early when three military officers carried out a coup (overthrow) of the government. The army, called the Haitian Guard, then backed Dumarsais Estimé, a black man, for president. Upon winning office, Estimé fired mulatto government officials and replaced them with blacks. He also carried out some social reforms, such as the formation of labor unions (associations of workers, who organize for higher pay and better working conditions).

In 1950 Haiti drafted a new constitution that called for the election of the president by a direct popular vote. In other words, the people, not the national assembly, would choose their own president. In 1951 Paul Magloire, a black army colonel, was the first president elected by popular vote. But Magloire's government was corrupt, and his opponents forced him out of office in 1956.

U.S. Marines pull out of Haiti in 1934. Following a successful democratic election and several years of stability in Haiti, the U.S. government relaxed its control of the nation.

Papa Doc and Baby Doc

On September 22, 1957, François Duvalier was elected president of Haiti for a six-year term. Nicknamed Papa Doc, Duvalier was a black physician and a leader in the Noirisme movement. A practitioner of Vodou, he was popular with the black middle class as well as the rural poor, but the mulatto elite considered him a threat to their status.

Once elected, Duvalier quickly moved to strengthen his grip on power. He attacked any group who opposed him. He banned labor strikes and rid the government and military of opposition party members. Using gangs of armed thugs, he threatened and imprisoned journalists and bombed and raided newspaper offices. Soon no newspapers or radios would dare to criticize him. Despite his terrorist tactics, many blacks supported Duvalier, who painted himself as a champion of the black masses.

But soon even Duvalier's supporters came to fear him. With the help of his aide Clément Barbot, Duvalier organized the National Security Volunteers, also called the Tontons Macoutes. Dressed in blue jackets, jeans, and sunglasses, with red kerchiefs around their necks, the Tontons Macoutes were, in fact, Duvalier's own private security force.

HAITI'S BOGEYMEN

The Tontons Macoutes, the dreaded security forces that terrorized Haitians during the Duvalier era, took their name from a Haitian folk figure, Tonton Macoute (Uncle Knapsack). In Haitian folklore, he carries off small children at night—sort of like the fictional bogeyman.

They tortured and assassinated Duvalier's opponents and terrorized ordinary Haitian citizens, using threats and violence to steal money and crops as they pleased. Fearing for their lives, thousands of Haitians—especially professional people who could afford to travel—fled the country during Duvalier's reign.

In 1964 Duvalier changed the Haitian constitution, making himself "president for life." In 1970 he changed the constitution again, this time lowering the age requirement for president so that his nineteen-year-old son, Jean-Claude (Baby Doc), could take over as president for life. Papa Doc died in April 1971. As planned, Baby Doc succeeded him.

Jean-Claude "Baby Doc" Duvalier and his father François "Papa Doc" Duvalier in the late 1960s. The Duvaliers governed Haiti with a harsh dictatorship for nearly three decades.

Jean-Claude's regime was not quite as harsh as that of his father. At first, he gave some freedoms to political parties, trade unions, and journalists. But worried about threats to his power, especially from upper-class mulattoes, Jean-Claude soon cracked down on the people once more. The Tontons Macoutes continued to terrorize Haitian citizens, especially Jean-Claude's political opponents. At the same time, Haiti's economy stalled. People began to go hungry.

Haitian professionals continued to move to other nations. Soon people from all economic backgrounds were trying to leave the country. Many traveled on overloaded, rickety boats, making their way to other Caribbean islands or to Florida in the United States.

Back in Haiti, resentment against the Duvalier dictatorship smoldered. Using radio to rally the masses, Catholic leaders condemned the government and called for justice, freedom, and democracy for Haiti's poor people. Finally, in May 1984, protesters took to the streets in Gonaïves, demonstrating against severe food shortages. Protests became larger and more frequent until, on February 7, 1986, Jean-Claude Duvalier and his family fled to France for their safety.

A New Leader

The army stepped in to restore order, naming Lieutenant General Henri Namphy as president. In 1987 his government wrote a new constitution for Haiti. But Namphy was just as corrupt as his predecessors, using the Tontons Macoutes to repress his opponents, especially the growing Catholic liberation theology movement (the church's effort to improve life for the poor). In September 1988, military leaders overthrew Namphy. Another general, Prosper Avril, took over as president. He, too, soon left office, fleeing the country in the face of popular protests and growing demonstrations.

> Throughout the mid- and late twentieth century, Haiti experienced a "brain drain," as educated professionals and businesspeople left the nation to escape brutal dictators. This exodus further weakened Haiti because it was left with fewer and fewer skilled people to run businesses, health clinics, government offices, and schools.

New elections were scheduled for 1990. An outspoken Catholic priest, Father Jean-Bertrand Aristide, decided to run for president. Young and charismatic, Aristide spoke about democracy and justice. He quickly gained widespread support in Haiti. In an election held on December 16, 1990, Aristide won the presidency with 67 percent of the vote.

Jean-Bertrand Aristide (front, center) promises a better financial and social future for Haitians during the 1990 presidential race in Haiti.

Aristide was sworn in on February 7, 1991. He promised reforms that would benefit Haiti's poor. But nine months later, an alliance of mulatto families and army generals—viewing the black Aristide as a threat to their wealth and power—overthrew Aristide's government. Aristide fled to the United States for safety.

Unhappy with the overthrow of a democratically elected president, the United States and the Organization of American States (an association of thirty-five countries in the Americas) imposed economic sanctions against Haiti's new government. That is, the nations limited trade with and financial assistance to Haiti to protest Aristide's ousting.

The sanctions put much strain on the already weak Haitian economy. The Haitian people grew even more desperate. Thousands risked their lives at sea to reach Miami, Florida. However, the U.S. Coast Guard intercepted most of the refugees, and the U.S. government—unwilling to care for thousands of poor Haitians—refused to allow them entrance into the United States. It sent some of the refugees to a U.S. military base in Cuba and returned the rest to Haiti.

U.S. president Bill Clinton felt that the best solution to the crisis in Haiti was to return Jean-Bertrand Aristide to the presidency. But Raoul Cédras, a general who had taken control in Haiti, refused to cooperate with the United States. What's more, Cédras had gangs of armed thugs harass and kill Aristide's supporters inside Haiti. So the United States imposed tougher sanctions, trying to put more pressure on Cédras—still with no results. Finally, in September 1994, the United States sent twenty thousand troops to see to it that President Aristide was allowed to return to power. With the backing of these soldiers, Aristide arrived in Haiti on October 15, 1994. General Cédras went into exile in Panama.

Continued Chaos

Upon returning to office, Aristide disbanded the Haitian military and replaced it with a less powerful police force. He wanted to run for office again in 1995, but the 1987 constitution forbid him from running for consecutive (back-to-back) terms. So his pre-coup prime minister, René Préval, ran instead, winning with 88 percent of the votes cast. Aristide remained active in politics, preparing for another run for president and promising to bring jobs, health care, education, and justice to Haiti's poor.

Haitians riot and loot food in Port-au-Prince in 1994. Haiti erupted in chaos as Aristide and General Raoul Cédras wrestled for power that year.

THE ARISTIDE CONTROVERSY

Jean-Bertrand Aristide's 2004 ouster caused controversy in the United States. Some Americans, particularly black members of the U.S. Congress, denounced the U.S. government for refusing to back Aristide. They charged that the United States had long been hostile to Aristide because his proposed economic reforms threatened U.S. business interests in Haiti. Some critics claimed that the United States had actually backed the anti-Aristide forces with weapons and money. The U.S. government, under President George W. Bush, refuted these charges. It cited the corruption, mismanagement, and abuses of the Aristide government as reasons for not backing Aristide.

In 2000 Aristide was reelected to office, despite fierce opposition from former army officers and other critics. Meanwhile, the Haitian people continued to suffer from poverty, unemployment, and hunger. And despite Aristide's promises of democratic and economic reforms, international observers accused his government of corruption, human rights abuses, and attacks on journalists and free speech. Once again, foreign groups placed economic sanctions on Haiti. The European Union, the United States, and international banks refused to give money to Haiti, hoping to pressure the Haitian government to make reforms.

By January 2004, opponents inside Haiti were calling for Aristide's immediate resignation. Violent protests erupted in the streets of Haiti, and rebel groups seized portions of the country. Aristide asked the international community—including the United States—for help, but foreign leaders had lost faith in him. He fled to safety in the Central African Republic and later South Africa.

Demonstrators protest the ousting of Haitian president Aristide outside the National Palace in Port-au-Prince on February 29, 2004.

With the violence swelling, in March 2004, several nations, including the United States, sent troops to Haiti to restore the peace. An interim government, headed by Boniface Alexander, chief justice of Haiti's supreme court, took over running the country. Later in the year, tragedy struck Haiti in the form of Hurricane Jeanne. The September 2004 storm killed nearly three thousand Haitians and left thousands more injured and homeless. It was a brutal blow for a nation that had already suffered so greatly.

Visit www.vgsbooks.com for links to information on Haiti's history and government. Find current news on the status of the country, its leaders, its people, and life after Aristide.

Government

According to its 1987 constitution, Haiti's chief executive is a president, elected by the voters to a five-year term. All citizens over the age of eighteen are eligible to vote. The president appoints a prime minister, who helps the president run the government.

Voters also elect a legislature, or national assembly. This body has two houses, a Senate and a Chamber of Deputies. The Senate has twenty-seven members, who serve six-year terms. The Chamber of Deputies has eighty-three members, who serve four-year terms.

The nation's court system consists of civil (noncriminal) and criminal courts, courts of appeal, and the Court of Cassation, which is the nation's supreme, or highest, court. The Haitian president appoints judges to their positions. For local governance, Haiti is divided into nine departments, which are further broken into wards.

THE PEOPLE

Haiti is home to approximately 8 million people. It has a population density of 747 people per square mile (295 per sq. km), making it one of the most densely populated nations in the Western Hemisphere. Haiti's population has grown rapidly in the last twenty years, and the high growth rate is expected to continue. The population is projected to reach 10.2 million in 2015.

Ethnic Groups

Blacks—descendants of African slaves—make up 95 percent of Haiti's population. The other 5 percent are mostly mulattoes—descendants of French planters and African slaves. Haiti also has a small population of Middle Easterners, descendants of Syrian and Lebanese people who came to Haiti in the nineteenth century, as well as Caucasians and people of other races. Historians believe that some black Haitians are descendants of Taíno Indians who intermarried with African slaves.

For most of Haiti's history, mulattoes have made up the elite, governing class in Haiti. Although they account for a small percentage of the population, they have owned most of the nation's businesses and held most of the political power. The majority blacks, on the other hand, have mostly been poor laborers or farmers, without much economic or political power. Several times in Haiti's history, such as during the Duvalier and Aristide regimes, small numbers of blacks have held powerful positions in government. Even during these years, however, most black Haitians remained poor.

Rural Life

About 79 percent of Haiti's people live in rural areas, mostly in the plains and valleys between Haiti's many mountain ranges. Most rural residents live in small villages and make their living by farming. Some make a living by fishing along the coast.

While many Haitians work on large, company-owned plantations, others cultivate small family farms, handed down from one generation to the next. The average family farm consists of two or three acres (about 1 hectare). On most farms, the soil is overworked and eroded. People use simple tools, such as shovels, picks, and hoes, to plant and harvest their crops. Most farmers grow maize (corn), rice, yams, beans, and tropical fruits. Some Haitian farmers own a few chickens, pigs, or goats, or perhaps a cow or mule. Typically, men perform the work of planting and harvesting crops, while women care for children and cook.

Most rural families are subsistence farmers. That is, they grow only enough food to feed themselves. Occasionally, families produce more food than they need. In that case, women of the family sell the surplus crops at a local market or trade them for household necessities, such as clothing or cooking utensils.

Most rural Haitian families live in small, two-room dwellings made of cinder blocks or wood. Most houses have no electricity or running water. People must gather water from rivers and wells. They cook outside over open fires. For fuel, they cut down trees to make charcoal.

⊙ Urban Life

In recent decades, many rural Haitians have left the countryside for the city. They have come seeking jobs, education, and decent housing.

Many of Haiti's poor crowd into urban neighborhoods, such as Cité Soleil in Port-au-Prince, hoping to find work and other necessities for survival.

Unfortunately, Haiti's big cities, Port-au-Prince and Cap Haïtien, have not been able to accommodate the newcomers from rural areas.

Many new arrivals crowd into slum areas such as Port-au-Prince's Cité Soleil, where they construct makeshift houses out of metal sheeting, bricks, and cardboard cases. Like homes in rural areas, these houses have no running water or plumbing systems. Residents must use outdoor drainage ditches as toilets. Those lucky enough to find jobs work in city factories, stores, and other businesses. But many people resort to begging to survive, while others turn to crime.

LIGHTS OUT

Haiti does not have reliable systems for producing and distributing electricity. As a result, most areas in Haiti have blackouts (shutting down of electric power) on and off during the day. During times with no power, some businesses use backup generators. Students read and study by candlelight or flashlight. People listen to battery-powered radios.

Outside of the slum neighborhoods, some urban Haitians occupy more comfortable homes. In Port-au-Prince, the wealthiest citizens—mostly mulattoes—live in Pétionville, an exclusive suburb filled with fine homes and even mansions. This neighborhood also houses upscale restaurants and shops. Wealthy city dwellers in Haiti generally work as business owners, politicians, doctors, or in other professional positions.

Health Issues

Because Haiti is a poor nation, most of its citizens don't receive high-quality health care. According to the World Health Organization, Haiti has only about eight doctors and ten nurses for every 100,000 inhabitants—one of the lowest such ratios in the world. Most of the nation's hospitals, health clinics, and doctors are found in urban areas, leaving rural dwellers with limited access to health care.

Life expectancy is low: just 50 years for men and 53 years for women. The infant mortality rate—the number of children who die within one year of birth—is high, at 74 deaths per 1,000 births. The maternal mortality rate (numbers of women who die around the time of childbirth) is also very high, with about 520 deaths per 100,000 births (compared to just 14 deaths per 100,000 births in the United States).

Only 54 percent of Haitians have access to sanitation facilities (toilets, indoor plumbing, and sewer systems), and less than half have a regular source of safe drinking water. Most rivers in Haiti are polluted with human and other waste. Diseases such as hookworm and typhoid, transmitted by contaminated food and water, are common in Haiti. In the spring of 2003, a typhoid outbreak in Haiti caused at least

THE EARLY AIDS SCARE

Doctors first identified AIDS in the early 1980s. Initially, the U.S. Centers for Disease Control and Prevention traced a number of AIDS cases to Haitian immigrants in the United States, then concluded that Haitians were at high risk for AIDS. The CDC later found that Haitians were no more at risk for AIDS than any other group, but the negative publicity hurt Haiti. Its small tourist industry suffered, as travelers fearful of AIDS shied away from Haiti. The drop in tourist business hurt Haiti's economy.

forty deaths and made hundreds sick. Malaria, transmitted by mosquitoes, is another widespread disease in Haiti. About half of Haiti's people suffer from malnutrition, or an insufficient diet, which weakens them and makes them vulnerable to infections.

One of the most serious health challenges facing Haitians is HIV, or the human immunodeficiency virus. This virus causes AIDS, or acquired immunodeficiency syndrome, a devastating and usually fatal illness. About 6 percent of adults in Haiti are HIV-positive, meaning they carry HIV. This rate of HIV infection is the highest in the Western Hemisphere. More than 30,000 Haitians have died of AIDS since the disease was identified in the early 1980s. The U.S. Centers for Disease Control and Prevention estimates that 200,000

This **medical poster** is part of a children's health education program in Haiti. The poster helps children understand how sickness can be transmitted by coughing. Haiti's medical system is one of the poorest in the world.

Haitian children have been made orphans due to the death of their parents from AIDS. However, many Haitians who carry the AIDS virus do not know they are infected.

Many Haitian and international health organizations are working to prevent and slow the spread of HIV and to treat Haitians who are already infected with the virus or sick with AIDS. This work is multifaceted. First, because HIV can be spread through sexual activity, AIDS workers are educating Haitian people about using condoms, which can prevent the spread of HIV during sex. HIV can also spread from a mother to a baby during the birth process. So AIDS workers are treating some HIV-positive pregnant women with drugs that can prevent this kind of transmission. Other workers distribute drugs that help people with AIDS live longer lives.

In July 2003, the U.S. government launched an AIDS prevention program in fourteen poor countries, including Haiti. This program, totaling $500 million in aid, focused on preventing mother-to-child HIV transmission, as well as providing AIDS education, testing, and treatment.

Education

Haiti has never had a good public education system. In French colonial days, planters had no interest in educating their slaves. Only whites and mulattoes received an education, many of them attending schools in France. Some young Haitians attended schools run by French Catholic priests, who mostly provided their students with religious training.

After independence, the mulatto elite opened a few schools in Haiti's cities. But there was no nationwide school system. In 1860 the Catholic Church sent additional French priests to teach young people in Haiti. Again, these priests focused their lessons on religious studies, as well as the French language and culture, and their students were largely wealthy mulattoes.

In the 1920s, during the U.S. occupation, the government opened some schools for adults in the Haitian countryside. These schools taught peasant farmers how to read and write, as well as farming techniques. In big cities, the government also opened vocational schools, which taught job skills to working people. More schools for children—many of them private religious schools—opened after World War II (1939–1945).

In the early 2000s, Haiti's educational system remains haphazard. Most schools (80 percent) are private, and many of them are run by religious groups. The remaining 20 percent of Haitian schools are state-run. Students learn their lessons in both French and Creole—the language of ordinary Haitians.

These Haitian children are going to class at a church-run school. They are in a minority. Fewer than half of Haitian children regularly go to school.

Many towns have no schools at all. Many classrooms are in disrepair and overcrowded, and communities have too few teachers and school buses. Most parents can't afford to pay for books, uniforms, and tuitions required by private schools. Other parents have their children work and help support the family rather than attend school. And Haiti has a large population of homeless children, who also do not attend school. Because of these obstacles, only about 40 percent of school-age children in Haiti regularly attend school. Only 53 percent of Haitian adults are literate—able to read and write.

The nation has only one university, the University of Haiti in Port-au-Prince, founded in 1944. Haiti also has several small private colleges. Many Haitians seeking a higher education—generally the children of the elite—avoid their own nation's schools, which aren't highly rated. Instead, these young people enroll in colleges and universities in France, the United States, and other nations.

Women and Children

Life is hard for almost everyone in Haiti. Roughly 80 percent of Haitians live in extreme poverty, and 70 percent do not have regular jobs. A lack of services such as health care, schooling, clean water, and electricity adds to the difficulty of day-to-day life. Although everyone suffers, Haitian women and children face the worst hardships.

By law, women and men have equal rights in Haiti. Women won the right to vote in 1957. Nevertheless, many women in Haiti suffer from discrimination and mistreatment. Many Haitian men physically abuse their wives and girlfriends, and the Haitian justice system rarely punishes men for such crimes. Women also endure sexual harassment and sexual abuse in the home and workplace.

Because jobs are so scarce in Haiti, women will generally take any work available. In cities many Haitian women toil in factories making goods for the U.S. market. The working conditions are unsafe, and the pay is rock bottom, but the employees are grateful to have jobs at all. Other women in Haiti resort to prostitution, or sex work, to earn money. Many sex workers are homeless teenagers.

The typical Haitian woman will have an average of five children in her lifetime. Because the Catholic Church discourages birth control, birth control pills and devices are not readily available in Haiti. Less than 20 percent of married women in Haiti use modern birth control methods, although some use herbal remedies to prevent pregnancy. Abortion is illegal in Haiti (except to save the life of the mother), so many women who want to end their pregnancies have abortions in secret, often from unskilled practitioners who use unsafe techniques. Many women die during these procedures.

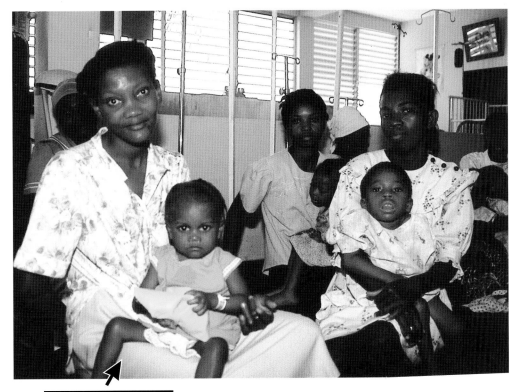

Women and children make up Haiti's poorest and most disempowered people. These mothers and their children are waiting for desperately needed health care at Grace Children's Hospital in Port-au-Prince.

Conditions for Haiti's children are even worse. Since so many families are poor, parents often need their children to work and help bring in income. Haitian law forbids children under the age of fifteen to hold jobs, and it sets rules about safe employment for older teenagers. However, child labor laws are rarely enforced in Haiti.

The U.S. Department of Labor estimates that more than 22 percent of Haitian children ages ten to fourteen were working in the early 2000s. They hold a variety of jobs, from factory work to farmwork to domestic service. Because the government does not monitor their employment, the child workers frequently suffer mistreatment at the hands of their employers. Their wages are meager, and their working conditions are sometimes dangerous.

Most human rights experts agree that the worst abuses of Haitian children involve young people called *restavecs*. They come from poor rural families, who send their children to work as household servants for urban families. The poor parents hope that host families will feed and educate their children in exchange for their labor. In reality, some host families physically and sexually abuse the restavecs. They are virtually slaves—without freedoms and with no payment for their labor.

These girls are former **restavecs, or child slaves.** The Maurice Sixto Center, an independent organization partnering with the United Nations, rescued the girls in the early 2000s. Visit www.vgsbooks.com to find links to more information about the people of Haiti.

Experts estimate that more than 300,000 Haitian children are living under such arrangements.

The U.S. Labor Department also estimates that from 5,000 to 10,000 children are homeless in Haiti. These youngsters live on the streets. Many resort to begging or prostitution for their survival. Other poor Haitian children are trafficked (shipped) to foreign countries, such as the Dominican Republic, where they are forced to work as prostitutes, farm laborers, or domestic servants. Like the restavecs, these children are essentially slaves to their employers.

CULTURAL LIFE

For many years, two cultures existed side by side in Haiti. One was the "official" culture promoted by the government, and the other was the culture of Haiti's ordinary people. For example, for more than 180 years after independence, Haiti's only official language was French, even though most Haitians spoke only Creole. It wasn't until 1987 that Creole was made an official Haitian language alongside French. Similarly, until 2003, Catholicism was Haiti's official religion. But most Haitian people practiced Vodou in addition to or instead of Catholicism. During Jean-Bertrand Aristide's second term, the government established Vodou as a state religion along with Catholicism.

⊙ Religion

Most Haitians (80 percent) practice the Catholic religion, which arrived in Haiti during French colonial days. Approximately 16 percent of Haitians subscribe to Protestant religions (Christian faiths that are distinct from Catholicism), and the remaining 4 percent belong to

other religions or do not practice any religion. But no matter what major faith they formally belong to, most Haitians also practice Vodou (also called voodoo), a religion with its roots in Africa.

Vodou is not unique to Haiti. Many people in the West Indies, Brazil (in South America), and West Africa practice different forms of Vodou. The religion originated in the African nations of Benin and the Congo. It arrived in the Western Hemisphere with African slaves. On Haiti, French masters and missionaries (religious teachers) taught their slaves about Catholicism. At the same time, the slaves secretly practiced Vodou. After independence, the Catholic Church and the Haitian government tried several times to outlaw Vodou. Church leaders denounced the religion as a sinister superstition. Politicians worried that Vodou priests might rally their followers to rise up against the government. Over the years, however, the Haitian government came to tolerate and accept Vodou as a valid religious practice. In 2003 Vodou joined Catholicism as a state religion.

A BAD RAP FROM HOLLYWOOD

Vodou, more commonly spelled voodoo, has gotten a bad reputation in the United States, largely due to old Hollywood movies that present a negative picture of the religion. Starting in the 1930s, horror movies with titles such as *Diabolical Dr. Voodoo*, *Voodoo Blood Bath*, and *Curse of the Voodoo* presented an outrageous and wildly distorted picture of Vodou as an evil practice featuring murderous zombies (people brought back from the dead).

In reality, Vodou is similar to religions found in many traditional societies around the world. Called animist religions, these faiths involve spirit and ancestor worship. In Haiti and other places where Vodou is practiced, worshippers sometimes welcome visitors to attend their ceremonies so that visitors can get a more accurate and positive image of Vodou.

The African word *voodoo* means "god," "spirit," or "sacred object." Followers of Vodou believe in one supreme god, called Gran Met (Great Master), and lesser spirits called Iwa. At formal ceremonies, people summon the Iwa using prayers, songs, drumming, and dancing. These spirits include Legba, the master of doorways and crossroads; Baron; the master of the dead; Erzulie Dantor, the goddess of love; Ogou, the god of war; and Agwe, master of the sea.

Over the generations, some elements of Catholicism and Vodou have been combined in Haiti. For instance, practitioners of Vodou use images of Catholic saints to represent their Iwa. Haitian funerals combine both Catholic religious rites and Vodou beliefs about death and the afterlife.

◉ Holidays and Festivals

Haitians celebrate secular (nonreligious) holidays, including Independence Day on January 1, Labor Day on May 1, and Armed Forces Day on November 18. They celebrate major Christian holidays such as Good Friday, Easter, and Christmas, and lesser holidays honoring important Catholic saints. Some holidays commemorate important events in Haitian history, such as the "discovery" of Hispaniola (by Christopher Columbus) on December 5 and the death of Jean-Jacques Dessalines on October 17.

Haitian holidays are usually festive events featuring lots of music, dance, and good food. Carnival, also called Mardi Gras, is held throughout the Caribbean world (and elsewhere) for three days leading up to Ash Wednesday, a Catholic holy day. Usually held in January or February, the celebration features bands, floats, and parades. Many celebrants

A Haitian man celebrates during Carnival by playing a drum. The drum is a traditional Haitian instrument with roots in Taíno and African cultures.

wear huge papier-mâché masks and dress like animals, devils, and fantastical beings. Rara, which follows Carnival, is another lively festival, again featuring bands and lots of good music.

Gédé, held on November 1 and 2, is also called All Saints' Day—a time to honor the spirits of one's ancestors. This holiday can be spooky, since it takes place in cemeteries. People wear black and purple clothing, light candles, and honor the Vodou god, Baron.

Music

Haitians enjoy a variety of musical forms, from Vodou drumming to Latin dance music and jazz. *Racines* (roots) music is a fusion of African, jazz, and traditional Vodou sounds. Haitians also enjoy Latin dance styles such as meringue (from the Dominican Republic) and *son* (from Cuba), as well as rap, hip-hop, and other popular music. Many Haitian songs are political—calling for the people to stand up against a repressive Haitian government and military.

Rara music, played during the pre-Easter Rara celebration, is a raucous sound performed with bamboo and tin trumpets, drums, maracas, and other percussion instruments. During Rara, bands of musicians parade through the streets on floats, accompanied by singers and dancers. The rara sound has its roots in Vodou ceremonies.

Kombites are rhythmic work songs, peppered with local news and gossip and sung in a lively tempo. Teams of farmers sing these songs in unison as they swing hoes and perform other labors. The music helps spur the workers on and makes physical labor more pleasurable.

The chief musical instrument of Haiti is the drum, which comes in a wide variety of sizes and shapes. Many Haitians also play guitars and accordions. Conch shells, called *lambis,* are large seashells that can be played like trumpets. Sometimes Haitians blow conch shells to round up neighbors for a work crew.

Language

Creole, the most widely spoken language in Haiti, is a blend of different languages—mostly French and various African languages. The language developed as Africans arrived in the New World as slaves. They brought their African words and language structures, adding French words learned from their white masters. Because English and Spanish pirates, sailors, and settlers were also active in the New World, some of their vocabulary got added to the mix. Creole speakers also picked up some words from the surviving Taíno Indians.

With Haitian independence, most French people were killed or driven out of Haiti. Creole-speaking blacks (former slaves) remained the majority in Haiti. Nevertheless, the minority mulattoes still spoke French, and they held positions of power in early Haiti. Official documents were written in French, and teachers gave their lessons in French. Since French was the language of the elite, poor Creole-speaking Haitians had difficulty participating in politics and business. This language divide deepened the gap between rich and poor.

MULTIPLE MEANINGS

The word *creole* has several different meanings. It refers to different kinds of languages: the Creole spoken in Haiti, also called Haitian Creole; a pidginized (simplified) version of French spoken by black people in southern Louisiana; or any pidginized language. *Creole* can also refer to different groups of people. People of European descent born in the West Indies or Latin America are called Creoles. People of mixed Spanish or French and African descent are sometimes also called Creoles. In the United States, the name Creole refers to descendants of French or Spanish settlers living in states around the Gulf of Mexico.

In the 1980s, black Haitians began a movement to increase the use of Creole in Haitian society. They won a major victory when Creole was made an official language of Haiti in the 1987 constitution. In modern times, the use of Creole in schools, the media, business, and government is on the rise. Some 90 percent of Haitians use Creole as their primary language, while the remaining 10 percent use French.

People who know French will recognize many French vocabulary words in Creole. For instance, *good morning* in French is *bonjour*. In Creole it's *bonjou*. *Stop* in French is *arrêter*. In Creole it's *rete*. The French word for *fish* is *poisson*. The Creole word is *pwason*.

Literature

The Taíno Indians, Haiti's original inhabitants, did not have a written language, nor did the Africans brought to Hispaniola to work as slaves. Slaves passed down their history and traditions through stories and songs. Griots, or storytellers, were important members of the black community both before and after independence.

The French masters, on the other hand, brought French literary traditions to Hispaniola. Priests and missionaries also used French to write about colonial life. After independence, educated Haitians continued to write about their nation in French.

At the turn of the twentieth century, Haitian writers began to describe the inequities in their nation—particularly the racial divide between blacks and mulattoes. Most of these writers had been educated in French-style schools, and they wrote their works in French.

During the Négritude movement of the mid-twentieth century, Haitian writers, still writing in French, celebrated their African identities. In 1927 a group of poets and novelists founded *La Revue Indigène* (Indigenous Review), a magazine dedicated to Haitian writing and Haiti's African heritage. Jean Price-Mars is famous for *Thus Spoke the Uncle* (1928), a scholarly book about Haitian music, folklore, and religious practices. Jacques Roumain wrote a book called *Masters of the Dew* in 1943. Considered one of Haiti's finest novels, it describes the hard life of Haitian workers and peasants. Other notable writers of the movement included the brothers Philippe and Pierre Thoby-Marcelin.

Haitian literature continued to thrive until François Duvalier took control of Haiti in 1957. Duvalier suppressed artwork, literature, and scholarship of all kinds. Many writers left the country during this era. From exile they wrote books criticizing Duvalier's government.

After the elder Duvalier died, the government of his son, Jean-Claude, gave writers and artists more freedom. Increasingly, Haitian writers incorporated Creole passages and dialogue into their works. In the twenty-first century, Haitian writers examine modern-day Haitian life as well as the lives of Haitian immigrants in other parts of North America. Well-known modern Haitian writers include Edwidge Danticat (who writes in English), Emile Ollivier (who writes in French), and Dany Laferrière (who also writes in French).

Visual Arts

Haiti is known worldwide for its vivid artwork. The first Haitian artists were not trained professionals. They were mostly Vodou practitioners who painted elaborate wall murals on temples and produced sequined flags for religious ceremonies.

In the early 1900s, U.S. artists took note of the colorful artworks emerging from Haiti, which the Americans termed "naive" or "primitive" because the Haitian artists were untrained. In 1944 DeWitt Peters, a U.S. artist and schoolteacher, opened the Centre d'Art (Art Center) in

This mural is Wilson Bigaud's *Miracle at Cana.* He created this famous work on a wall of the Holy Trinity Cathedral in Port-au-Prince, painting from 1950 to 1951.

Port-au-Prince, hoping to encourage Haitian painters. The response was great, as hundreds of untrained beginners poured in from the mountains and city slums to take lessons in oil painting. Three years later, Peters showed their works at the International Exhibition in Paris. By the late 1940s, Haitian paintings were in great demand in the art galleries of New York City.

In 1949 the Art Center arranged for Haitian artists to paint huge murals in Haitian cathedrals (large churches) and on the walls of hotels, airports, and other buildings. The most magnificent of these murals, *Miracle at Cana,* was created by Wilson Bigaud. It depicts scenes from the Bible placed in a Haitian setting. That mural and others adorn the walls of the Episcopal Cathedral of the Holy Trinity in Port-au-Prince.

In the twenty-first century, Haitian craftspeople have taken center stage. Gabriel Bien-Aimé, Serge Jolimeau, and others—known as the Blacksmiths of Vodou—are metalworkers who make fanciful sculptures from oil drums and old cars. Haitian woodworkers use rich tropical woods to produce striking carved figures. Other craftspeople make papier-mâché animals and delicate hand-painted boxes.

Filmmaking

Movie companies rarely shoot Hollywood films in Haiti. The nation is considered too dangerous and politically unstable for movie production. However, Haitian-born filmmaker Raoul Peck has made several small-budget fictional films about Haitian life. In addition, many documentary (nonfiction) films have been made in and about Haiti. *Bitter Cane* examines Haiti's desperate economic system. *Abandoned* looks at the plight of Haitian immigrants in the United States, and *Rezistans* deals with the struggle for democracy in Haiti.

Acclaimed U.S. filmmaker Jonathan Demme has made two documentary films about Haiti. His *Dreams of Democracy* (1988) looks at Haiti after the overthrow of the Jean-Claude Duvalier regime. *The Agronomist* (2004) examines the life and murder of Jean Dominique, head of Radio Haiti Inter, a station that has long rallied the country's poor people to fight against injustice and oppression.

Food

At expensive hotels and restaurants, diners can order fancy French foods in Haiti. But almost everywhere else, people eat Creole dishes. Haitian Creole cooking features rice, beans, and potatoes; mangoes, plantains (similar to bananas), and other fruits; meat and seafood; and spicy sauces. Lunch is the biggest meal of the day. Visitors can buy lots of tasty dishes from street vendors and small cafés.

CREOLE SHRIMP

This spicy dish is served over white rice. Follow the directions on a package of rice, and cook enough for six servings.

3 tablespoons butter

¼ cup chopped green pepper

½ cup chopped onion

1 cup celery, chopped finely

1 clove garlic, peeled and minced

2 cups canned tomatoes

1 can (8 ounces) tomato sauce

½ cup water

1 teaspoon Dijon mustard

½ teaspoon sugar

dash Tabasco sauce

1 teaspoon salt

⅛ teaspoon pepper

1 bay leaf

1 pound cooked shrimp (available at supermarket fish counters and frozen food aisles)

1. In a sauté pan, melt butter over low heat.
2. Add pepper, onion, celery, and garlic. Cook over medium heat until vegetables turn golden brown.
3. Add tomatoes, tomato sauce, water, mustard, sugar, Tabasco, salt, pepper, and bay leaf. Cook 20 to 25 more minutes, stirring often.
4. Add shrimp and cook 10 minutes longer.
5. Remove bay leaf. Serve over rice.

Serves 6

Some common Haitian dishes are *diri ak pwa* (rice and beans), *bannann peze* (fried plantains), *tasso* (jerked beef), *griyo* (fried pork), *kabri* (goat), and lambi (conch). *Ti malice* is a sauce made of onions and herbs. *Jomou* soup is a tasty pumpkin soup. Rum, made from locally grown sugarcane, is a favorite drink in Haiti. Locally produced coffee is another popular drink.

Sports and Recreation

Soccer is the most popular sport in Haiti. Many towns have local clubs and frequent pickup games. Haiti's national soccer league has more than fifty teams. Many matches take place in the Sylvio Cator Stadium in Port-au-Prince. When relaxing with friends and family, people often play Krik? Krak! This is a popular traditional game of riddles and storytelling. Dominoes is a favorite board game. Like people in most countries, Haitians enjoy watching television, listening to music, and going to the movies in their free time.

Boys play **soccer** at school during recess. Most Haitians are avid soccer fans and follow Haitian teams with great pride.

Visitors to Haiti can enjoy diving and snorkeling in the surrounding ocean waters. They can even explore underwater shipwrecks from colonial days. People can also hike and bird-watch in Haiti's national parks. Generally, such outdoor activities are more popular with tourists than with ordinary Haitians.

Find links to more information about Haitian Vodou, arts, cuisine, current events, and sports at www.vgsbooks.com.

THE ECONOMY

Haiti is the poorest country in the Western Hemisphere. The nation's economic problems include severe inflation (rapidly rising prices), a trade deficit (the country imports more goods than its exports), and a lack of foreign investment. Haiti must import much of the food, petroleum, clothing, medicines, and other basic materials that its people need. Its entire annual budget, $300 million, is less than that of many small cities in the United States. Since the 1980s, its economy has shrunk steadily (producing fewer goods and services each year than the year before).

About 80 percent of the population lives in poverty. More than two-thirds of eligible workers do not have regular jobs. Many Haitians work as subsistence farmers, raising just enough food to feed their families. Others work in the informal sector—which involves the buying and selling of goods and services without government oversight or regulation. The typical worker makes only about US$480 per year.

Not everyone in Haiti is poor, however. Approximately 1 percent of the population owns more than 50 percent of the nation's wealth.

Wealthy Haitians enjoy fine homes, expensive cars, and other luxuries. The economic inequality causes resentment among the nation's poor and has often led to popular uprisings.

For many years, Haiti has relied on aid from foreign nations and loans from international agencies such as the World Bank. But several times in the 1900s and again in 2000, the United States and other groups imposed sanctions, or economic penalties, on Haiti. Foreign observers charged the Haitian government with corruption, economic mismanagement, and human rights abuses. For instance, in the late 1990s, the United States claimed that corrupt government officials were stealing most of the U.S. aid money sent to Haiti, rather than using it for improvement projects such as building roads and schools. By cutting off economic aid, foreign groups hoped to pressure Haiti's government into making reforms. Despite sanctions, Haiti still receives large amounts of economic aid from humanitarian groups, such as the U.S. Agency for International Development.

Tourists sun themselves on a beach near Port-au-Prince. Ongoing political and social unrest have brought Haitian tourism to nearly a halt.

Services

The service sector, which includes health care, banking, communications, education, tourism, government, and sales, accounts for 50 percent of Haiti's gross domestic product (GDP—the value of all goods and services produced in a nation in one year). About 25 percent of Haiti's workers are employed in the service sector.

Like most of Haiti's economy, this sector is not particularly strong. All the industries that make up the service sector, such as health care, education, and communications, are weak and struggling, without enough money to adequately serve the nation. Because Haiti has a history of violence and political unrest, many tourists avoid Haiti, choosing to visit the adjacent Dominican Republic or neighboring Caribbean islands instead. So the tourist industry struggles as well.

HAITIAN INVESTMENT

An estimated 1.5 million Haitians live outside the country, mostly in Miami, New York, Boston, and Montreal. About 300,000 Haitian immigrants live in Florida alone. These Haitians often send money home to help their families in Haiti. By some estimates, Haitians living abroad send more than $300 million (almost one-fourth of Haiti's GDP) back to Haiti each year.

Agriculture

Farming is the second-largest sector of the Haitian economy, accounting for 30 percent of GDP. About 66 percent of Haitians work as farmers, many cultivating small two- or three-acre (1-hectare) plots, which they rent or own. Other farm laborers work on large plantations operated by foreign companies.

Haitian farmers grow a variety of crops, including corn, rice, beans, plantains, bananas, mangoes, and sugarcane. Some farmers raise livestock such as pigs, cows, and chickens. Coffee, cocoa (made from cacao beans), and animal and vegetable oils are the biggest farm exports. The nation also has small forestry and fishing industries.

Industry

Industry is the smallest sector of the Haitian economy, accounting for 20 percent of GDP. Only about 9 percent of the workforce is employed in this sector. Haitian factories produce clothing, sporting goods (including baseballs), electronic parts, chemicals, cement, and other products. Some plants refine sugar, mill flour, and process other farm goods. Haiti has a small mining industry.

A Haitian farmer works a field using a plow pulled by oxen.

The United States is Haiti's biggest trade partner. More than half of Haitian imports comes from the United States, and more than 80 percent of its exports go to the United States. Haiti also does small amounts of business with Canada, the Dominican Republic, and other Caribbean nations.

Many foreign companies operate factories in Haiti. For instance, the Walt Disney Company manufactures children's clothing in Haiti. Critics charge that many foreign-owned factories are unsafe and dirty, without proper ventilation (clean, circulating air) or bathroom facilities for the workers. Pay is also very low—the typical worker makes only $2.75 per day. But because jobs are scarce in Haiti, many workers are afraid to speak out against unfair labor practices. They worry that if they protest or try to organize labor unions, they will be fired.

The Black Market

With so much poverty and so few jobs, it is not surprising that many Haitians turn to illegal activity to make money. The illegal economy is called the black market. Haiti is a hub for the trafficking (large-scale sale and shipping) of illegal drugs—especially cocaine—between South and Central America, Europe, and the United States. Observers charge

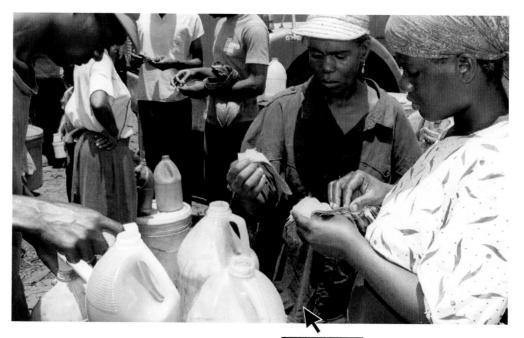

These Haitians are buying gasoline on the **black market.** In short supply, gas brings a high price, costing about US$9.00 a gallon. Visit www.vgsbooks.com to find links to more information about the Haitian economy.

Most Haitians use ***taptaps* (brightly painted buses and trucks)** for transportation. Owning a car is a luxury most Haitians cannot afford.

that even Haiti's government is involved in the illegal drug trade, with high-ranking judges, police officers, and politicians taking a share of drug profits in exchange for allowing traffickers to operate in the country. Some Haitians even traffic human laborers, especially children, into the Dominican Republic and other parts of the Caribbean.

Transportation

Haiti has 2,583 miles (4,160 km) of highways. Only 628 miles (1,011 km) of those roads are paved, however. Many mountain roads become choked with mud and impassable in wet weather. Haiti's best road is a two-lane highway that stretches for 200 miles (322 km) through the mountains between Port-au-Prince and Cap Haïtien.

Very few Haitians—fewer than 5 out of 1,000—own cars. In the cities, people frequently take communal (group) taxis and colorfully painted public buses called taptaps. There is no railroad in Haiti. People take rickety buses from city to city. They sometimes travel by mule or on foot.

Haiti has twelve airports—only three of which have paved runways. Port-au-Prince has an international airport, opened in 1965, with daily flights to Miami, Montreal, New York, Panama City, Paris, and various cities in the Caribbean. Cap Haïtien and Port-au-Prince are Haiti's principal shipping ports.

Communications

Haiti's telephone system is poor. Phone lines often go out of service, making it impossible for users to place calls. Few Haitians have home telephones. Some homes and businesses use party lines, or shared telephone lines. Small numbers of Haitians have cell phones.

Internet cafés operate in Haiti's big cities, and about eighty thousand Haitians are Internet users. The vast majority of Haitians, however, cannot afford to buy or use computers. Limited electrical and phone service also make it impossible for most Haitians to use the Internet.

The nation has dozens of radio stations and three TV stations, providing a variety of news, sports, and entertainment programs. Most stations broadcast in Creole as well as French. Since electricity does not run twenty-four hours a day in Haiti, many people use battery-powered televisions and radios.

Most newspapers in Haiti are published in French. These appeal to the educated, French-speaking elite. *Le Matin* and *Le Nouvelliste* are daily French-language papers. *Haiti Progrès* and *Haiti en Marche* are French-language weeklies. A few papers are published in Creole, the language of most Haitians. *Libète,* published weekly, is the most widely read Creole newspaper.

The Future

If the past is any indication, Haiti's future will be a difficult one. Its new government, set up after Jean-Bertrand Aristide's departure, faces

Volunteers build a home as part of **a housing project** in Haiti. Such projects offer hope for Haitians and are essential to a better future for Haiti.

the long-standing problems of poverty, unemployment, homelessness, AIDS, crime, and political unrest. Hurricane Jeanne, which struck in fall 2004, has only deepened the misery for the people of Haiti.

The new government is trying to win back the favor of the World Bank and other international lenders by reforming its economic policies. If the government can show sound and honest economic operations, international organizations will likely resume lending large amounts of money to Haiti for projects such as roads, schools, health care, and sanitation systems.

Meanwhile, many foreign governments and humanitarian groups are working to improve life for Haitian people. For instance, the American Friends Service Committee, affiliated with the Quaker religion, has undertaken a reforestation (tree-planting) program to help restore Haiti's forests and to combat soil erosion. The U.S. Agency for International Development is working with Haitian farmers to improve crop yields and working with Haitian businesses to better their chances of success. The U.S. government began its AIDS prevention program in Haiti in 2003.

THE REFUGEE DILEMMA

In 2003 the U.S. Coast Guard picked up approximately two thousand Haitians trying to reach U.S. shores in boats. However, the refugees were not allowed to enter the United States and were sent back to Haiti. Critics charge that U.S. policy toward Haitian refugees is racially biased. They note that the United States is quick to admit lighter-skinned Caribbean refugees, specifically those escaping from the dictatorship in nearby Cuba.

The U.S. government argues that its refugee is not based on race. It admits Cuban refugees, it says, because they are fleeing political repression in Communist Cuba. The political situation in Haiti does not fit the U.S. guidelines for admitting refugees.

Ultimately, however, Haiti's recovery will need to come from within. If the nation can improve its governance, health care, and educational and business systems, it could begin to generate more jobs, homes, and wealth for its people. The first two hundred years of independence have been troubled ones for Haiti. The Haitian people—and indeed the whole world—hope that the next two hundred years will be brighter.

C. 2600 B.C.	Native American people migrate from Venezuela to the Caribbean Islands, including Hispaniola.
C. 250 B.C.	The Saladoids, a different group of native people from Venezuela, arrive in the West Indies.
C. 100 B.C.	The Taíno Indians, originating in either Peru or Venezuela, settle in the West Indies.
A.D. 1492	Explorer Christopher Columbus, with an expedition of three ships, encounters several Caribbean islands, including Hispaniola.
1493	Columbus establishes the settlement of La Isabela on Hispaniola's northern coast.
1520s	The first African slaves arrive in Hispaniola.
1630	French and British pirates take control of Tortuga Island.
1664	France takes control of the western part of Hispaniola.
1670	French settlers found Cap Haïtien (originally Cap-François) on Hispaniola's northern coast.
1749	French settlers found Port-au-Prince in the Gulf of Gonâve.
1791	Mulattoes and slaves revolt against the French colonial government.
1803	Local black and mulatto fighters defeat French forces at the Battle of Vertières.
1804	Haiti declares its independence.
1806	An assassin kills Jean-Jacques Dessalines, independent Haiti's first ruler.
1807	Henri Christophe takes control of northern Haiti, and Alexandre Pétion becomes president of southern Haiti.
1808	The eastern portion of Hispaniola, the modern-day Dominican Republic, returns to Spanish control.
1820	Jean-Pierre Boyer becomes the leader of a unified Haiti.
1821	Haitian troops conquer eastern Hispaniola from the Spanish.
1843	Boyer flees Haiti to avoid a popular rebellion. People in eastern Hispaniola throw off Haitian rule, establishing the Dominican Republic.
1915	The United States sends marines to Haiti to establish stability and protect U.S. business interests.
1920s	Black Haitians begin the Négritude movement.

1934   The United States pulls the marines out of Haiti.

1944   The University of Haiti and the Centre d'Art open in Port-au-Prince.

1957   François Duvalier, nicknamed Papa Doc, is elected president of Haiti. He rules as a dictator.

1965   An international airport opens in Port-au-Prince.

1971   Jean-Claude Duvalier (son of François) succeeds his father as president, also ruling as a dictator.

1986   Facing a popular uprising, Jean-Claude Duvalier flees to France.

1987   Creole becomes an official language of Haiti alongside French.

1990   Jean-Bertrand Aristide, a Catholic priest, is elected president of Haiti.

1991   Jean-Bertrand Aristide is overthrown and flees to the United States for safety. The United States and other nations place economic sanctions on the new Haitian government.

1994   Backed by U.S. soldiers, Aristide returns to the presidency in Haiti.

1998   The United Confederation of Taíno People forms to honor and promote Taíno culture.

2000   Aristide is reelected to office. The United States and international organizations again place sanctions on Haiti, in hopes of pressuring Aristide to make reforms.

2003   The U.S. government launches an AIDS prevention program in Haiti and thirteen other poor countries. Vodou joins Catholicism as an official religion of Haiti.

2004   Haiti marks its two-hundredth anniversary of independence. Facing a popular uprising, Aristide resigns the presidency. Hurricane Jeanne hits Haiti, killing nearly three thousand people.

2005   Haiti schedules the first presidential election since the ousting of Aristide.

COUNTRY NAME: Republic of Haiti

AREA: 10,714 square miles (27,749 sq. km)

MAIN LANDFORMS: Massif du Nord, Noires Mountains, Massif de la Hotte, Massif de la Selle, Artibonite River valley, Cul-de-Sac Plain, Central Plain, North Plain

HIGHEST POINT: Mount la Selle (8,793 feet or 2,680 m)

LOWEST POINT: sea level

MAJOR RIVERS: Artibonite, Les Trois

ANIMALS: alligators, barracudas, crocodiles, egrets, flamingos, guinea hens, lobsters, parrots, rhino-horned iguanas, scorpions, sea turtles

CAPITAL CITY: Port-au-Prince

OTHER MAJOR CITIES: Cap Haïtien, Gonaïves, Jacmel, Jérémie, Les Cayes, Miragoâne, Port-de-Paix, Saint-Marc

OFFICIAL LANGUAGES: French, Creole

MONETARY UNIT: gourde. 1 gourde = 100 centimes.

(Side tab: Currency | Fast Facts)

CURRENCY

Haiti's unit of currency is the gourde. In 1807, only a few years after independence, President Henri Christophe wanted to build up the nation's money supply. At the time, people used gourds—the hard husks of the calabash fruit—as bowls and utensils. Christophe had soldiers travel from village to village collecting gourds. He amassed more than 200,000 of them. He declared the gourds to be money and used them to pay peasants for their coffee crops, which he then sold to European merchants for gold. Thus gourds enabled Haiti to establish a gold-based currency, and Haiti's official unit of money became called the gourde.

The Haitian government issues 1- and 5-gourde coins and 1-, 2-, 5-, 10-, 25-, 50-, 100-, 250-, and 500-gourde notes (paper money). The gourde is divided into 100 centimes, and 36 gourdes equal approximately one U.S. dollar.

Jean-Jacques Dessalines, Haiti's first ruler, created the nation's flag. In 1803, as blacks and mulattoes were struggling for independence from France, he grabbed a red, white, and blue French flag and ripped out the white stripe—claiming to be ripping white people from the nation. Then he had the red and blue halves sewn together. Thus the modern Haitian flag has a blue stripe and a red stripe. Blue stands for the blacks of Haiti, and red stands for the mulattoes. Haiti's coat of arms sits in a box in the center of the flag.

Haiti's national anthem, "La Dessalinienne" ("The Dessalines Song") is named for Jean-Jacques Dessalines, the nation's first ruler. The anthem was written on the occasion of Haiti's one-hundred-year anniversary. Justin Lhérisson wrote the words, and Nicolas Geffrard wrote the music. The song was written in French, but it is also sung in Creole. Here are some of the English lyrics:

> Let us be masters of our soil
> United let us march
> For our country
> For our forefathers
>
> For our forebears
> For our country
> Let us toil joyfully
> May the fields be fertile
> And our souls take courage.
> Let us toil joyfully
> For our forebears,
> For our country.

Visit www.vgsbooks.com for links to websites with additional information about the Haitian national anthem, "La Dessalinienne."

Flag National Anthem

ANACAONA (1474–1502) Born in Yaguana (modern-day Léogâne), Anacaona was a famous Taíno Indian. Her brother ruled over one Taíno kingdom, and her husband ruled another. In 1494 Christopher Columbus's troops kidnapped her husband. Anacaona fled to her brother's kingdom and took over his power, ruling as queen. Called the Golden Flower, she was famed for composing songs and ballads and was greatly loved by her subjects. In 1502 the new Spanish governor of Hispaniola had his troops kill many of Anacaona's people. She was killed by hanging.

JEAN-BERTRAND ARISTIDE (b. 1953) Aristide was born in the town of Port-Salut but grew up in the slums of Port-au-Prince. He became an ordained Catholic priest in 1982 and studied for a time in Canada. He returned to Haiti in 1985 and worked as a priest in a slum area of Port-au-Prince. There, he founded a center for homeless street children and preached liberation theology over the radio, gaining a widespread following among the Haitian poor. Running with his Lavalas Party, he won a landslide victory in Haiti's 1990 presidential election. After only eight months, however, a military coup removed him from office. He spent three years in exile in the United States before U.S. troops returned him to the Haitian presidency. Aristide ran for president again in 2000 and again won by a vast majority. However, opponents forced Aristide from office once more in 2004. This time, he took refuge in Africa.

JEAN-MICHEL BASQUIAT (1960–1988) The son of a Haitian father and a Puerto Rican mother, Basquiat was born in New York City. As a teenager, he became known as a talented graffiti artist. He also made paintings, which caught the attention of Andy Warhol and other leaders in the art world. Museums, galleries, and collectors rushed to buy his works, propelling him to international fame. In 1988, at the age of twenty-seven, Basquiat died of a drug overdose. A 1996 Hollywood movie, *Basquiat,* told the story of his short life and career.

GARCELLE BEAUVAIS (b. 1966) A model and actress, Beauvais was born in Saint-Marc and moved with her family to Massachusetts at the age of seven. At the age of sixteen, she began a modeling career, appearing in advertisements and fashion spreads in magazines such as *Ebony* and *Essence.* She also walked the runway during fashion shows. In 1990 she began an acting career, winning roles on *Models Inc., NYPD Blue,* and other television shows. She has also appeared in several films.

EDWIDGE DANTICAT (b. 1969) A native of Port-au-Prince, novelist Danticat migrated to New York with her family at the age of twelve. Her first novel, *Breath, Eyes, Memory* (1994), tells the story of a Haitian immigrant girl in the United States. In 1995 Danticat was a National Book Award finalist for a short-story collection, *Krik? Krak!*

She has received numerous other literary awards, including the 1995 Pushcart Short Story Prize. Her most recent novel is *The Dew Breaker* (2004). In 2005 she published a children's book about the famous Taíno queen Anacaona.

HECTOR HYPPOLITE (1894–1948) Hyppolite, born in Saint-Marc, is considered the first great Haitian painter. A self-taught artist and a Vodou priest, Hyppolite made his early paintings with homemade paintbrushes made of chicken feathers. His work was discovered by American schoolteacher DeWitt Peters, who saw Hyppolite's painting of birds and flowers on a café door in Haiti. Hyppolite then joined Peters at the Centre D'Art in Port-au-Prince. He quickly achieved international fame for his paintings, many of which featured images of Vodou ceremonies and spirits.

WYCLEF JEAN (b. 1970) Musician and singer Jean was born in Croix-des-Bouquets and moved to Port-au-Prince as a small child. When he was nine, he moved with his family to New York. As a young man, Jean formed the hip-hop trio the Fugees, who produced several CDs, including the highly acclaimed *The Score*. In 1997 Jean released his first solo album, *Wyclef Jean Presents the Carnival*, which included four songs in Creole. His most recent album is *Welcome to Haiti: Creole 101*, released in August 2004.

GARRY PIERRE-PIERRE (b. 1962) Born in Port-au-Prince, Pierre-Pierre moved to the United States at the age of eight. He studied journalism at Florida A&M University, then embarked on a newspaper career. He worked for many years at the *New York Times* and other U.S. papers, covering news in both the United States and Haiti and earning numerous awards for his reporting. In 1999 Pierre-Pierre left the *New York Times* to start the *Haitian Times*, a weekly English-language newspaper geared toward the Haitian American community. The paper covers events and issues in both the United States and Haiti.

FRANÇOIS-DOMINIQUE TOUSSAINT (1743–1803) Born a slave on a plantation in northern Haiti, François-Dominique Toussaint (also known as Toussaint-Louverture) grew up to lead the Haitian revolution against France. Unlike most slaves, Toussaint learned to read and write as a boy. He held positions of responsibility on the plantation, and, as was sometimes done, his master gave him his freedom in 1791. In 1792 he joined the Haitian slave uprising and soon became its leader. After the French agreed to give all slaves their freedom, Toussaint led French forces fighting Spain and Great Britain on Hispaniola. He became ruler of the French colony, but the French soon grew angry with Toussaint. Agreeing to meet for a peace treaty, the French instead had him captured and sent to prison in France, where he soon died.

THE CITADEL Overlooking Cap Haïtien to the north, the Citadel is a vast mountaintop fortress built over a period of fifteen years. Haitian ruler Henri Christophe had the structure created during his reign in the early nineteenth century. The fortress has towering walls that measure 13 feet (4 m) in thickness. Recently restored, the Citadel once housed five thousand troops plus Christophe's family. The views from the site are sensational.

CORMIER BEACH A popular beach resort on Haiti's northern coast, Cormier is also an excellent spot for diving and snorkeling. In addition to coral reefs and underwater caves, divers can explore seventeenth- and eighteenth-century wrecks of Dutch, French, and Spanish ships.

MARCHÉ DE FER This enormous marketplace in Port-au-Prince, built in 1889, features a fanciful Arabian-style design. Inside, the market is packed with vendors selling food, spices, household goods, and items used in Vodou worship. Artists and craftspeople also create and sell their work in the loud, colorful market.

MUSEUM OF HAITIAN ART The works of Haiti's great naive painters, including Hector Hyppolite, are permanently exhibited at this Port-au-Prince museum. The museum also rotates shows of contemporary Haitian painters, photographers, and other artists.

NATIONAL MUSEUM This museum in Port-au-Prince traces centuries of Haitian history, beginning with the Taíno Indians and following through to modern times. Visitors can see many historic artifacts, such as an anchor from the *Santa María,* Christopher Columbus's flagship.

SANS SOUCI Sans Souci was a magnificent early nineteenth-century palace south of Cap Haïtien. Henri Christophe had the palace built between 1810 and 1813. He conducted royal business there until his death in 1820. In 1842 an earthquake hit Cap Haïtien and the surrounding region, seriously damaging the palace. Nevertheless, its ruins are still spectacular to visit.

TROU CAÏMAN This lake northeast of Port-au-Prince is a great spot to view waterbirds, including flamingos, herons, ibis, and ducks. Raptors such as falcons sometimes make their homes here as well. The lake's name means "alligator hole," but alligators no longer live here.

LA VISITE NATIONAL PARK Located in the western Massif de la Selle, this park includes limestone caves, stunning waterfalls, and cloud forests (forests so high in the mountains that they are usually shrouded in clouds). The park is popular with foreign hikers.

colony: an area ruled by a distant nation

corruption: wrongdoing in government or business

coup: the overthrow of a government, often by violence

deforestation: the widespread destruction of forest lands, usually by logging

dictator: a leader who holds absolute control over a nation and often rules oppressively

endangered species: a type of plant or animal that is in danger of dying out completely

epidemic: a widespread outbreak of disease

erosion: the wearing away of rock or soil, usually by the water or wind

exile: a period of forced absence from one's home country

gross domestic product: the value of all goods and services produced in a nation in one year

hydroelectricity: electric power created by the force of rushing water

immigrant: someone who arrives to live in a new country

indigenous: native to a particular place

irrigation: a network of channels, pipes, and other structures, designed to carry water to crops

liberation theology: a religious movement for justice and equality on behalf of the poor

missionary: a religious teacher who tries to convert others to his or her faith

mulatto: a person of mixed black and white ancestry

privateer: a pirate who operates with government consent

refugee: a person who flees his or her country to escape danger or persecution

regime: the government of a specific leader or group

sanctions: economic restrictions imposed by nations and intended to pressure other governments to make changes

subsistence farming: growing only enough crops to feed one's family, with nothing left over to sell

tropical: describing a region of the earth near the equator with year-round high temperatures, rainfall, and plant growth

Glossary

Selected Bibliography

Arthur, Charles. *Haiti in Focus: A Guide to the People, Politics, and Culture.* **Northampton, MA: Interlink Publishing Group, 2002.**
This comprehensive guide explores Haitian geography, history, culture and society. It examines the many troubles facing the Haitian economy and government.

Central Intelligence Agency (CIA). "Haiti." *The World Factbook,* **2004.**
http://www.cia.gov/cia/publications/factbook/geos/ha.html (2005).
Compiled by the Central Intelligence Agency, this website gives basic statistical data on Haiti, with sections on government, economy, geography, people, and more.

"Country Profile: Haiti." *BBC News.* **2004.**
http://news.bbc.co.uk/1/hi/world/Americas/country_profiles/1202772.stm (2005).
This extensive site, produced by the British Broadcasting Corporation, offers current news stories from Haiti, profiles of Haiti's leaders, a historical timeline, statistics, and other information.

Doggett, Scott, and Joyce Connolly. *Dominican Republic and Haiti.* **2nd ed. Melbourne: Lonely Planet Publications, 2002.**
This guidebook for travelers examines Hispaniola as a whole and then describes the island's two nations, the Dominican Republic and Haiti. The authors provide information on Haitian history, culture, and society, with specific details for foreign visitors.

Farmer, Paul. *The Uses of Haiti.* **Monroe, ME: Common Courage Press, 2003.**
This scholarly work explores how Haiti's people have suffered from injustice and inequality and how U.S. government policy has contributed to the suffering in Haiti.

Goodman, Amy, ed. *Getting Haiti Right This Time: The U.S. and the Coup.* **Monroe, ME: Common Courage Press, 2004.**
This title looks at the recent ouster of Jean-Bertrand Aristide in Haiti and questions U.S. involvement in the Haitian government. Various authors, including U.S. political activist Noam Chomsky, contribute chapters.

"Haiti: A Country Study." *Library of Congress.* **1989.**
http://llcweb2.loc.gov/frd/cs/httoc.html (2005).
This site provides a good, thorough overview of Haitian history, government, and society through the late twentieth century.

"Haiti." *World Health Organization.* **2004**
http://www.who.int/countries/hti/en/ (2005).
On this site, the World Health Organization provides statistics on health care and health issues in Haiti, with information on disease outbreaks and prevention, health care professionals, and general health indicators.

"Indepth: Haiti." *CBC News.* **2004.**
http://www.cbc.ca/news/background/Haiti (2005).
The Canadian Broadcasting Corporation created this site, which offers analysis of Haitian politics and history, as well as information on current events.

Rotberg, Robert I. *Haiti: The Politics of Squalor.* **Boston: Houghton Mifflin Company, 1971.**
This book offers a comprehensive history of Haiti, from independence through the mid-twentieth century.

Wilentz, Amy. *The Rainy Season: Haiti since Duvalier.* **New York: Touchstone, 1989.**
The author provides a firsthand look at Haitian society at the end of the Jean-Claude Duvalier regime. She offers insights into the nation's history, the lives of its people, the movement for social justice, and the Vodou religion.

Danticat, Edwidge. *Anacaona, Golden Flower, Haiti, 1490.* **New York: Scholastic Inc., 2005.**
Danticat, an acclaimed Haitian novelist, tells the story of the famous Taíno queen, who perished at the hands of the Spanish, along with most of her people.

Discover Haiti.
http://www.discoverhaiti.com
This site offers information on all things Haitian, with sections on culture, history, and sights for travelers.

Embassy of the Republic of Haiti in Washington
http://www.haiti.org
Through this site, the Haitian Embassy provides a variety of material on Haiti—from business to government to cultural information.

Haitian Times Online Edition
http://www.haitiantimes.com
Published in New York, this weekly paper offers news for the Haitian community in the United States. It includes sections on news, art and culture, health, and more, with coverage of events in both Haiti and the United States.

Haiti Support Group
http://haitisupport.gn.apc.org
This site offers a wealth of information on Haitian life and culture, with sections on art, famous Haitians, current events, and more.

Hinz, Martin. *Haiti.* **New York: Children's Press, 1998.**
This title examines Haiti's geography, history, culture, and society. Colorful illustrations augment the text.

Kaufman, Cheryl Davidson. *Cooking the Caribbean Way.* **Minneapolis: Lerner Publications Company, 2002.**
This cookbook offers readers a sampling of recipes for dishes found in Haiti, the Dominican Republic, and throughout the Caribbean region.

Myers, Walter Dean. *Toussaint L'ouverture: The Fight for Haiti's Freedom.* **New York: Simon and Schuster Children's Publishing, 1996.**
This biography for young people is illustrated with paintings by Jacob Lawrence, a black American artist from the 1930s. Through words and dramatic pictures, the book chronicles Toussaint's life and the struggle for Haitian independence.

Ngcheong-Lum, Roseline. *Haiti.* **Milwaukee: Gareth Stevens Publishing, 1999.**
This attractive book examines Haitian life and culture through its various festivals, including Carnival, Mardi Gras, and All Saints' Day. Readers will also learn about Haitian arts, crafts, religion, and national heroes.

Temple, Frances. *Taste of Salt: A Story of Modern Haiti.* **New York: HarperTrophy, 1994.**
This novel for young readers tells the story of seventeen-year-old Djo, who experiences brutality and despair in modern Haiti. Inspired by the teachings of Jean-Bertrand Aristide, Djo remains hopeful for a happier future in his homeland.

Further Reading and Websites

vgsbooks.com
http://www.vgsbooks.com

Visit vgsbooks.com, the homepage of the Visual Geography Series®. You can get linked to all sorts of useful online information, including geographical, historical, demographic, cultural, and economic websites. The vgsbooks.com site is a great resource for late-breaking news and statistics.

Yurnet-Thomas, Mirta. *A Taste of Haiti.* New York: Hippocrene Books, 2002.

This cookbook offers more than one hundred Haitian recipes, ranging from meat dishes to drinks to desserts. Information on Haiti's history and holidays is included. Recipes are provided in English, Creole, and French.

Captions for photos appearing on cover and chapter openers:

Cover: Two fishing boats off the western coast of Haiti. Fishing is a small industry in Haiti. Most fishers catch only enough fish to feed their familes.

pp. 4–5 Two women carrying bundles of handwoven baskets stop on their way to market to pose for a picture.

pp. 8–9 This is an aerial view of Cap Haïtien. The northern Haitian city is situated between the Atlantic Ocean and the foothills of the Massif du Nord mountains, east of Acule Bay.

pp. 18–19 A Haitian girl looks at ancient pictographs (picture language) created by Taíno Indians. Evidence such as these pictographs indicate that the Taíno peoples had a thriving culture long before the arrival of Europeans in the 1400s.

pp. 38–39 Men work a rice paddy (field) in the Artibonite River valley. Traditionally in Haitian farming families, men plant and harvest crops.

pp. 48–49 This oil painting shows a Vodou (Voodoo) religious ceremony. The painting has a distinctively Haitian style called naive. Naive painters are formally untrained, but their art is rich and masterful. Vodou is a blending of traditional western African and Catholic faiths.

pp. 58–59 Haitians go about their day in an impoverished area of Port-au-Prince. The Haitian economy is weak and benefits only a few. Most Haitians live in poverty.

Photo Acknowledgments

The images in this book are used with the permission of: © Ask Images/Art Directors, pp. 4-5; Ron Bell/Digital Cartographics, pp. 6, 11; © Sophia Paris/UN/MINUSTAH/Reuters/CORBIS, p. 7; © Kay Shaw, pp. 8-9, 13, 16-17, 40, 42, 44, 45, 58-59, 63, 64; © Tony Arruza/CORBIS, p. 10; © Joe McDonald/CORBIS, p. 14; © Stephanie Maze/CORBIS, pp. 18-19; © Bettmann/CORBIS, pp. 20-21, 25, 31, 32; Library of Congress, pp. 23 (LC-USZ62-134204), 26 (LC-USZ62-7863); © Hulton Archive/Getty Images, p. 24; Schomburg Center for Research in Black Culture, pp. 27 (SC-CN-99-0010), 28 (SC-CN-99-0009); © Les Stone/CORBIS, p. 34; © Peter Turnley/CORBIS, p. 35; © Benjamin Lowy/CORBIS, p. 36; © Marc French/Panos Pictures, pp. 38-39, 57, 60; © Robert Nicklesberg/Time Life Pictures/Getty Images, p. 46; © Earl Young/Art Directors, pp. 48-49; © Savino Tony/CORBIS SYGMA, p. 51; © Jean-Leo Dugast/Panos Pictures, p. 54; © Sean Sprague/Panos Pictures, p. 61; © Thony Belizaire/AFP/Getty Images, p. 62 Audrius Tomonis—www.banknotes.com

Front Cover: © Marc French/Panos Pictures. Back Cover: NASA